Specimens
of
Piles.

Collected by J. A. Warne

Department Nº 2

Piles of Lower Animals

Vol. IX.

HAIR

Calcareous
XIII.

Department
Piles of
Lower Anim
V. 10.

Specimens of Hair

The Curious Collection
of Peter A. Browne

Doctor Benjⁱⁿ Rush

signer of the Decⁿ of Independence

Specimens of Hair

The Curious Collection of Peter A. Browne

Robert McCracken Peck

Photographs by Rosamond Purcell

Blast Books
NEW YORK

Specimens of Hair: The Curious Collection of Peter A. Browne
Published by Blast Books
P.O. Box 51, Cooper Station
New York, NY 10276-0051
www.blastbooks.com

Photographs from the collections of the Academy of Natural Sciences
of Drexel University by Rosamond Purcell

Edited and designed by Laura Lindgren

Set in Scotch Text

ISBN 978-0-922233-49-6

Library of Congress in Publication Control Number: 2018032991

Printed on 115 gsm Kasadaka White in China through Asia Pacific Offset

First Edition 2018

10 9 8 7 6 5 4 3 2 1

It is wisdom to profit by the errors of others.

—Peter A. Browne
Trichologia Mammalium, 1853

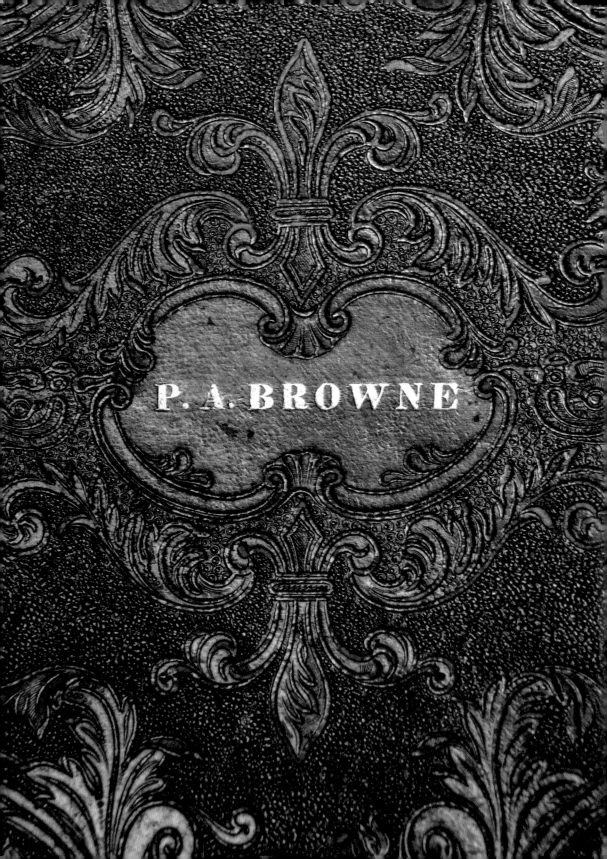

CONTENTS

INTRODUCTION

Museums are conspicuous showplaces and secretive treasure troves, centers for hands-on study and guardians of objects so fragile that unprotected they could not survive. Since its founding in 1812, The Academy of Natural Sciences of Philadelphia (now part of Drexel University) has gathered scientific objects for both study and display. In all, eighteen million natural history specimens, all carefully cataloged, are tended by the museum's scientific departments and kept under tightly controlled temperature and humidity conditions to shield them from the ravages of time. Among the Academy's treasured collections are the first dinosaur skeleton ever articulated and mounted for public display (1868), most of the plants Lewis and Clark collected on their historic journey across North America (1804–1806), Thomas Jefferson's personal fossil collection (once kept at the White House), John James Audubon's famous double elephant folio of North American birds (1827–1838), and several hundred of the bird specimens Audubon collected in 1843 during his last great expedition to the Yellowstone River.

Also in the Academy's archive is a peculiar nineteenth-century collection of hair, wool, and fur—the topic of this book and one of the Academy's least-known holdings. The Peter A. Browne collection of pile, as its creator called it, was deeded to the museum by Mr. Browne in 1860. In recent time, it has emerged from a century and a half of obscurity to become the focus of national and international attention. But it is thanks only to a pure fluke that Mr. Browne's remarkable collection was not lost forever. This is the story of the pile collection's creation, its rescue from destruction, and its significance today as a unique record of the diversity of life.

In 1976, when I began my curatorial career at the Academy of Natural Sciences, the institution was in the midst of physical upheaval. Many of its scientific research collections were being moved out of the building that had a century before been built to keep them, and into a newly acquired building half a mile away, to make more room for the Academy's public museum. Our new home was to be the onetime headquarters for the Reliance Insurance Company, an art deco gem appealingly located across the street from the Philadelphia Museum of Art and the city's beloved Azalea Garden. The planned expansion to occupy two buildings proved financially stressful, and the decision to divide the Academy's research and exhibition in two was soon reversed. We eventually moved everything back to our Logan Square headquarters and the abandoned art deco building was taken over by the PMA, but at the time I arrived, the relocation of our core collections into a brand-new space meant the Academy was abuzz, especially behind the scenes.

Relocation inevitably entails disposal, and at the Academy lots of things were being thrown away. One day, less than a month into my new role as assistant to the director of the museum, as I was still finding my way through the maze of hallways in our nineteenth-century building, I happened upon a large, disheveled pile of papers and three or four old, scuffed metal boxes, all marked for disposal. They were set on the floor outside a row of offices whose occupants I'd not yet met but whose names I recognized from the staff list.

The discarded administrative files were of no real interest, but eyeing the sturdy metal boxes I wondered why they should be doomed to the dumpster. Imagining how I could repurpose them, maybe to store my notebooks and papers, or maybe stack them up to make a bedside table in my new, still unfurnished apartment, I decided that I would rescue these intriguing, slightly tarnished and battered objects and put them to good use.

When I picked up one of the boxes to examine its construction and gauge its weight, I was surprised to discover it was not empty. Inside was a yellowing, marbleized paper-covered scrapbook filled with pages embellished with various decorative border frames surrounding ribboned tufts of hair affixed to the pages. Leafing through the bulky book, I instantly understood that this was not the personal detritus of a museum employee. What I held in my hands was the thoughtful work of a diligent collector from another time who had intended this assemblage for some scientific purpose. Each box held one or more albums of similar format, and each album's pages were filled with meticulous handwritten identifications of the hair, wool, and fur specimens displayed.

Looking for someone to tell of the alarming mistake I thought I had discovered, I knocked on the doors of a couple of nearby offices. Surely whoever set the boxes out for disposal couldn't have realized what was in them. Few of the people I spoke with seemed to know or care about the boxes I had found. Those who knew what I was asking about dismissed my concern, saying that the contents of the boxes were of no value to the Academy and were being removed to make room for more relevant things. Realizing I was determined to save the boxes and their contents, one of my new colleagues led me down the hall to the curator who had decided their fate.

A tall, distinguished gentleman who appeared to be in his seventies politely greeted me and invited me into his well-appointed office. I introduced myself as the new assistant to the director of the Academy's museum and explained what I had found; surely a mistake had been made in setting the boxes out for disposal in the trash rather than relocation to the other building. His grimace made clear that he was well aware of what I was talking about and that no error had been made. This was a collection he wanted nothing to do with. "We don't study hair at the Academy," he tersely explained. "I can't imagine why we ever took in such junk in the first place. It's not a scientific collection; it's just a bunch of scrapbooks with clippings of hair."

"You really intend to throw it away?" I asked incredulously.

"Of course!" he replied. "Someone should have done so years ago. What's in those albums is quite disgusting, and certainly of no use to anyone from a scientific point of view. Those boxes have been taking up valuable space for far too long, and we have many more important things to focus on. I checked some years ago with the Academy's library, and no one there seems to want them either."

"Could I take them?" I asked.

"Please do," he said. His tone of voice indicated that the topic was now closed; the page had been turned on the tin boxes and their contents. I thanked him for his time and the unexpected

National
Pile
6.

Eccentrically
elliptical.

Limited

HAIR

Miscellaneous.
Vol. VIII

gift. He wished me well in my new job, shook my hand, and returned to his desk, no doubt wondering what sort of oddball the Academy had just hired. Clearly I would require tutoring to learn the difference between useless clutter and the pursuit of science.

Astonished by the outcome of our conversation, I returned to the hallway discards and with a large black marker boldly added *NOT* above the word *TRASH* scrawled at the top of the scraps of paper taped to each box. I continued on my walk through the building, marveling at my good fortune and trying to absorb the meaning of it all.

By the time I returned with a cart in the afternoon, the elderly curator and his colleagues had left for the day. The janitor had removed the piles of administrative papers but, happily, the old tin boxes and their mysterious contents remained.

I took the boxes and placed them in a large storage cabinet in my new office, and there they remained for a number of years. Later, when I was asked to move my office from one part of the Academy to another, I decided that something more formal should be done with the albums. I approached the institution's archivist about adding them to the library's treasures. Her research into the files revealed an earlier memo from the curator prior to his deaccessioning of the albums (to me). In it he had speculated on the possible value—monetary, not scientific—of the collection. He had simply been trying to decide what to do with it. It was unclear from his note just where the boxes were at the time or who was in charge of their care, but it was evident he did not want to be. The Browne pile had fallen between the cracks. It was not really an archival collection in the traditional sense, nor was it considered to have any value for scientific research. Perhaps that was the very moment when their fate was set until, by sheer chance, I entered the picture.

Fortunately, the archivist I had approached, a successor to the archivist the curator had consulted years before, was sympathetic to my argument that the collection I had salvaged deserved and needed protection and that the Academy archives should become its permanent home. I was greatly relieved when she accepted the collection on behalf of the library.

Years later, while writing about some early scientific expeditions in which the Academy was involved, I noticed that some of the names that came up in my research were names that I remembered seeing with the wool and hair samples in the Browne albums. When I went to examine the albums again to confirm my recollection, I was distressed to discover that although the albums were intact, they had been transferred to archival storage boxes. The metal boxes that had initially drawn my eye had been discarded after all. Had I only known of any question about archivally sound storage for the albums, I could have saved both the boxes and their contents! Still, at least the albums and their precious historical contents had been preserved.

A couple of decades passed before I renewed my contact with the Browne collection. In 2008, as part of a temporary exhibition mounted for Presidents' Day weekend, I organized a small display of some of the most notable pages in Mr. Browne's albums. For just three days, locks from George Washington, Thomas Jefferson, James Madison, and a few other White House residents were shown in a wooden case in the Academy's library. The response was overwhelming: newspapers across the country

P. A. BROWNE'S COLLECTION OF PILE.

Prof. Samuel G. Morton
Philad.ª

Samuel George Morton

and around the world picked up stories from AP, UPI, and Reuters, and I received interview requests from the press, ranging from National Public Radio's *All Things Considered* to Radio New Zealand. Everyone wanted to know about the curious collection. Eight years later, with the Democratic National Convention being held in Philadelphia, I was asked to reprise the presidential hair display. The press response was even greater than before, leading to a flurry of requests to see the rest of the collection.

Of all the responses we received to the hair exhibit, the most gratifying came from former president Jimmy Carter. I had written to him, as well as to all of the other living presidents, to invite them to see the display when they were in Philadelphia for the convention. I had closed my invitation with a suggestion that we would be pleased to add a sample of their own hair to the collection. I didn't really expect any replies, but to my delight President Carter answered a few weeks later with a handwritten note saying that he would not be attending the Philadelphia convention but would be happy to donate a sample of his hair. The only problem, he explained, was that recent cancer treatment had resulted in his hair being quite short. What did I advise?

I quickly replied that a lock of his hair at any length would be most welcome and that we would be even more pleased if he might be willing to tell us something about it. Many weeks passed with no response, and I became convinced that Mr. Carter, or perhaps his staff, had second thoughts about my odd request. Then an envelope bearing the return address of the Carter Center in Atlanta arrived. Inside was a small plastic bag containing snippets of silvery hair accompanied by a note: "I had a military haircut at the Naval Academy and during my years in submarines.

His Excellency,

John D. Adams.

Later, before and during my presidential years, I wore my hair much longer than now. Since returning home from the White House, I have kept it cut quite short, so these pieces are mostly less than one-half inches long. I did not anticipate growing longer locks for display in a museum!"

Thanks to Jimmy Carter, a new twenty-first-century life has been breathed into the collection that Peter Browne began more than 170 years ago. There are, no doubt, many scientific purposes to which the Browne collection's contents can be applied in the future, many of which we might not be able to imagine now, just as scientists of the nineteenth century could not imagine the discoveries that lay ahead. For now, the Academy maintains the collection as a marvel to ponder and enjoy. It seemed fitting that we disseminate the collection in the form of a book with photography by Rosamond Purcell, the dean of natural history specimen photography, with whom both Laura Lindgren, the publisher, editor, and designer of this volume, and I had worked several times. To our delight, she agreed to participate, and together we pored through the albums so meticulously assembled by the country's most disciplined and devoted hair collector. In keeping with her hallmark practice, Rosamond made her photographs using natural light, moving the albums from windowsill to windowsill throughout the Academy's 140-year-old building, beautifully capturing their spirit and physical appearance.

In preparation for this book and to better understand the Browne collection, my research into the topic of collected hair has taken me from Italy, where hair relics from various saints have long been preserved and honored by the Catholic Church, to Mount

Vernon, the home of America's own sainted patriarch, which holds countless hair samples from the president and his family. Hair samples in libraries, archives, museums, and historic houses from Maine to Florida and from the East Coast to West reveal a widespread exchange of hair samples in the United States through the eighteenth and nineteenth centuries, but also how very unusual the Browne collection was for its time and remains today. Not a gathering of a few specimens from next of kin or famous celebrities, it is a methodical, systematic collection of every type of hair, human and animal, from every part of the world. The story behind the collection, bound to provide information for generations to come, is as mysterious as it is fascinating.

P. A. BROWNE'S COLLECTION OF PILE.

The Emperor
    Gen.' Napoleon Bonapart.

given by the English
surgeon at St. Hel
-ena to I K M

DUCIT AMOR PATRIÆ.

THE PILE ALBUMS
OF PETER A. BROWNE

Interest in hair, human and otherwise, runs as deep into time as anything in our DNA. From the practical to impractical—warmth, identity, spiritual meaning, style—the significance of hair has always been elemental. For one nineteenth-century collector, it became an all-consuming subject of scientific fascination. In the turbulent decades of the 1840s and '50s, as America struggled to stabilize its democracy and establish its place in the world, Peter Arrell Browne (1782–1860), a Philadelphia lawyer and naturalist, tried to understand this nation of immigrants by looking at its hair. The donors to the collection he formed, some willing, some not, ranged from well-known artists, writers, and scientists to dwarfs, giants, and the insane. They also included judges, governors, senators, congressmen, and thirteen of the first fourteen presidents of the United States.

Browne pursued his remarkable assemblage not for sentiment's sake or as a gathering of celebrity souvenirs, but to supply keys to a number of scientific puzzles he was eager to solve. A patriotic man, Browne was committed to building what he called a "national collection" of something he knew few others had studied, despite its widespread appeal. After focusing his energy on geology, botany, and a range of other natural history topics, he devoted the last third of his life to exploring mysterious patterns

PREFACE.

NATURAL HISTORY includes *all* the works of the Mighty Creator; her votaries, with the aid of the telescope, measure the parallax of the most distant stars, and, with the microscope, scrutinize the minutest portion of the smallest infusoria, plant, or crystal. Nothing for them is too large, nothing too small for examination, which God has placed within their reach. If the Deity has not deemed it beneath *His* dignity to *create* an object, surely it would be presumptive in man to consider it too insignificant for *his* study. Then let no one marvel that we have devoted so much time to ascertain the organization, properties and uses of hair and wool. To the unreflecting, this department of knowledge may, at first view, appear to be trifling; but, with each successive advance, it will acquire more importance.

The Science which relates to Pile may be called TRICHOLOGY, (from Trix, a hair;) its descriptive part is TRICHOGRAPHY. It is a branch of Zoölogy, or rather of Mammology; and, so far, it is connected with Physiology, Anatomy and Comparative Anatomy. Some of its discoveries shed new light upon the ethnological problem of the unity of the human species, and others will be found to be intimately connected with those branches of agricultural industry, which relate to the raising of Sheep and producing of wool, and the raising of Swine for the bristles. It embraces a large field of inquiry, many parts of which are yet only partially explored.

In our progress we have endured considerable mental labor and encountered some unexpected difficulties; but, cheered by the countenance and aided by a few scientific friends, we have pursued a steady course, and have, at length, brought our examinations to a tolerably successful termination. It will be recollected that we were obliged, in the first instance, to collect the *materials;* and, after years of untiring exertions, we have at length the largest and the most valuable known cabinet of pile. In the meantime we attended lectures on Physiology and Anatomy. We have made use of none but superior instruments, and some of these are entirely new—either in themselves or their application to this study. We have availed ourselves of the researches of those who have gone over the ground before us, at all times acknowledging their truthfulness and pointing out their errors. We have carefully preserved the specimens from which our drawings are made, for future re-examination, if desirable. Upon a theme so extensive, and comparatively so novel, we do not expect to have escaped error; but we trust that when pointed out, we shall ever be found ready to acknowledge and correct them.

P. A. BROWNE,
Philadelphia.

The preface to Browne's *Trichologia Mammalium* (1853)

The English Sheep.
McCully list of British Sheep.

Names of the Breeds.				Weight of Fleece.	Wethers per Quarter.	Age killed.
				lbs.	lbs.	Years.
1. Teeswater	No horns	White face and legs	Long wool	9	30	2
2. Lincoln	No horns	White face and legs	Long wool	11	25	2
3. New Leicester	No horns	White face and legs	Long wool (fine)	8	22	2
4. Cotswold	No horns	White face and legs	Long wool (fine)	9	24	2
5. Romney Marsh	No horns	White face and legs	Long wool (fine)	8	22	2
6. Dartmoor or Bramton	No horns	White face and legs	Long wool (fine)	9	25	2
7. Exmoor	Horned	White face and legs	Long wool (coarse)	6	16	2½
8. Heath	Horned	Black face and legs	Long wool (coarse)	3	15	3½
9. Hereford, Ryland	No horns	White face and legs	Short wool (fine)	2½	14	3½
10. Morf, Shropshire	Horned	Black and speckled	Short wool (fine)	1¾	12	3½
11. Dorset	Horned	White and speckled	Short wool (fine)	3½	18	2
12. Wilts	Horned	White and speckled	Short (midd.)	3	20	3
13. Berks	No horns	Black and white	Long wool	7	18	2½
14. South Down	No horns	Speckled and white	Short wool	2½	18	2
15. Norfolk	Horned	Black and white	Short wool	2	18	3½
16. Herdwick	Horned	Speckled and white	Short wool	2	10	4½
17. Cheviot	No horns	White face and legs	Short wool	3	16	4½
18. Dun-faced	No horns	Dun face and legs	Short wool	1½	7	4½
19. Shetland	No horns	Various-coloured ditto	Fine cottony	1¾	3	4½
20. Spanish	Rams horned	White	Short wool (super)	3½	14	2½
21. Ditto, cross			Ditto fine	2¾	16	2

in the natural world with the keratin-based substance he called "pile."[1] It was work he believed would serve his country in a variety of useful ways.

COLLECTING FOR SCIENCE

Peter Browne began his unusual research not with human hair, but with sheep wool and a microscopic analysis of its structure that he hoped would advance agricultural practices in the United States. Using wool samples he gathered from around the world and a special instrument he invented to measure the relative strength and elasticity of each, he determined which sheep breeds would be best suited for the fabrication of different commercial products, from felt hats to woven blankets.[2] Ultimately, he divided all sheep into two types, "hairy" and "wooly." He then explained to the growers and the people who used their product why wooly sheep were the best type to turn to for "the manufacture of felts and all cloths which *are required to full* [to be milled]," whereas hairy sheep produced fleece ideal for "the manufacture of flannel, worsted, blankets, hose, and all articles that are required *not to shrink*."[3] The relative advantages of different kinds of wool had been noticed by generations of cloth manufacturers and tailors, but Browne was the first person to explain the reasons for these differences.

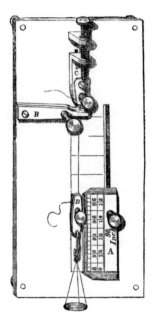

Browne's trichometer

The word he created to describe his hair and fleece study was "trichology," from *trikhos*, the Greek word for hair,[4] and he dubbed the instrument he invented to test the "ductility, elasticity and tenacity" of wool fibers a "trichometer."[5] In 1849 the Philadelphia Society for Promoting Agriculture declared his measuring device "essential" to the manufacture of wool products and lauded it for enabling farmers "to select the best wooled sheep with much more certainty than can be done by the eye or hand alone, consequently to improve their flocks by rejecting those of inferior quality."[6] A Philadelphia newspaper was equally enthusiastic, reporting that "Mr. Browne's invention furnishes the wool grower with the certain means of making the selection of breeders best calculated to increase the value of fleece, with scarcely any expense, expenditure of time, or scientific information."[7]

Although Browne was not a sheep breeder himself and appears not to have benefited financially from the exhaustive

P. A. BROWNE'S COLLECTION OF PILE.

There are two species of Sheep, viz

1 The Hairy Sheep &

2 The Woolly Sheep.

There is, perhaps, a 3rd Species, bearing both hair & wool

The Hairy Sheep.

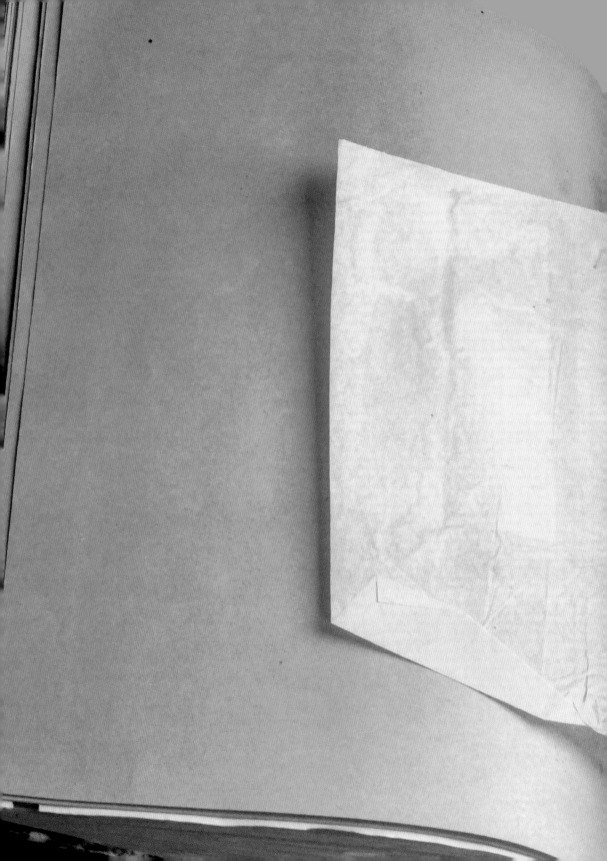

P. A. BROWNE'S COLLECTION OF PILE.

DUCIT AMOR PATRIÆ.

study of wool he undertook, his deep knowledge and many contributions to the field were well respected by the agricultural community worldwide.[8] In 1851 he was invited to submit some of his American wool samples for display at the Crystal Palace Exhibition in London.[9] Other parts of his collection were later included in a "universal trade-museum" in England.[10] In 1852 the Farmers Club of Pennsylvania declared his the best assemblage of such fibrous productions "that has ever been seen in the United States,"[11] a description still fitting more than 165 years later.[12]

ANIMAL HAIR

Browne's success with the study of sheep wool soon evolved into a study of wool, fleece, fur, and hair from mammal species well beyond sheep. With the help of willing correspondents in Europe, Asia, Africa, South America, and across North America, Browne filled album after album—what he called his "cabinets"—with samples of proven or potentially useful animal pile. He gathered hair from goats, camels, horses, yaks, bears, elephants, llamas, rabbits, beavers, otters, and giraffes. Even mouse, squirrel, and shrew fur came under his analytical gaze. He found that every different kind of pile, whether "grown upon ordinary [domestic] animals, or the covering of any extraordinary [wild] mammal," had a distinctive structure, essential in predicting its potential use to man.[13] "Hair, wool and fur are objects of great utility in manufactures and the arts," he wrote, "and their study cannot, therefore, fail to excite general interest, especially in this country, where the history of every thing that can increase the wealth of the nation, or add to the comfort, or even to the luxury,

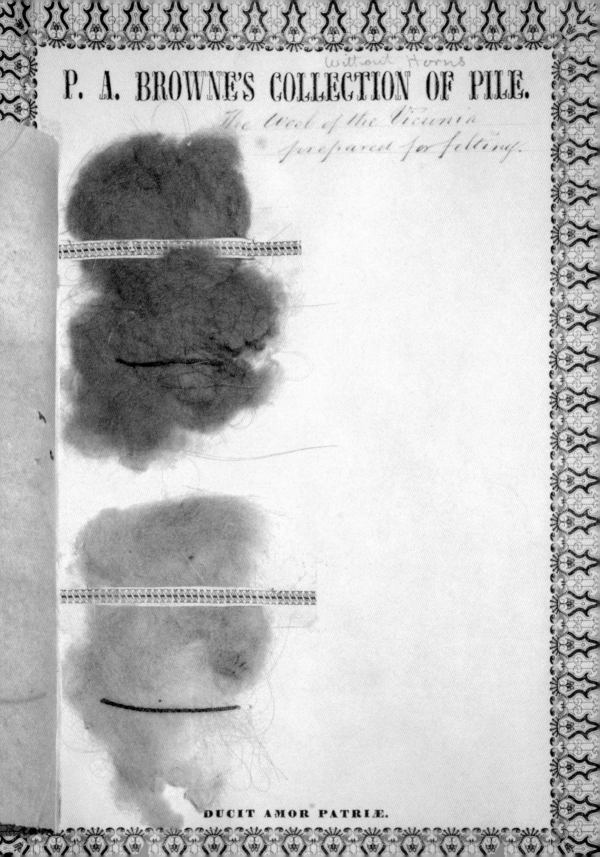

P. A. BROWNE'S COLLECTION OF PILE.

Without Horns

The Wool of the Vicunia
prepared for felting.

DUCIT AMOR PATRIÆ.

Fleece of the Thibet Goat
from the Zoological Gar-
den, London.

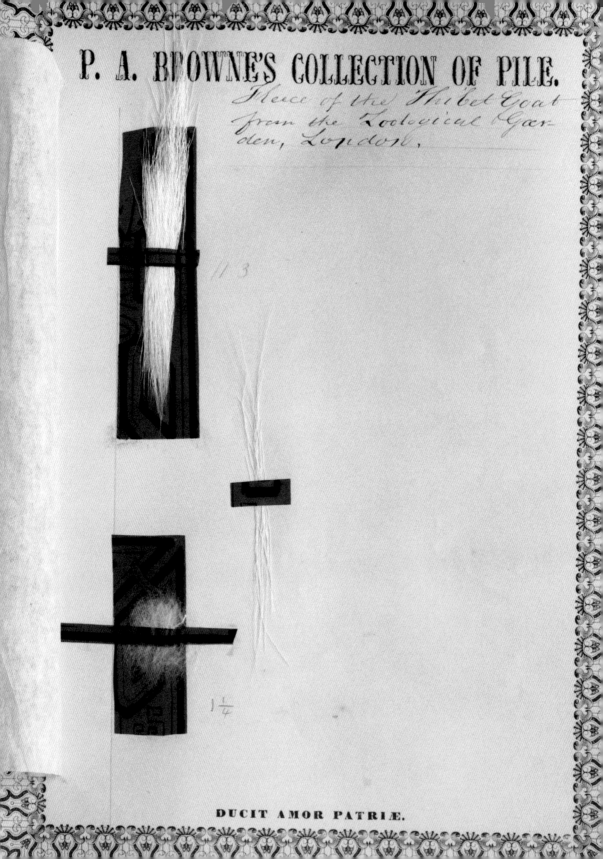

1½ 3

1 ¼

of people, is a legitimate object of pursuit."[14] He hoped that such a study also might shed light on how various species were related to each other and to the natural order of life, subjects not fully understood in a pre-Darwinian world.

For his self-published *Trichologia Mammalium, Or a Treatise on the Organization, Properties and Uses of Hair and Wool, Together with an Essay Upon the Raising and Breeding of Sheep* (1853), Browne used his trichometer to calculate the weight, ductility, and elasticity of the hair of a sloth, an elk, a grizzly bear, and "the stomach of a ruminant." He added the "spine of the peccary" and an "elephant's beard" for good measure.[15] No one had ever thought of making detailed measurements of these things before.

In the first half of the nineteenth century, animal fur was more commonly used in manufacturing than it is today. "The hair of some of the lower animals, such as the Horse, Ox, &c., is used to increase the tenacity of plastering mortar," he noted in *Trichologia Mammalium*. "The hair of the tail and mane of the Horse has long been woven into a cloth, extensively used in covering sofas and chairs," he continued. "It is also used for making sieves."[16] In the same publication, he provided a list of thirty-seven wild animals whose hair he said was in common use in North America. They were:

The Buffalo, the Bear, the Leopard, the Dog, the Raccoon, the Badger, the Glutton, the Skunk, the Polecat, the Fitch or Ferret, the Weasel, the Ermine, the Marten, the Sable, the Mink, the Otter, the Beaver, the Wolf, the Fox, the Jackal, the Jenet, the Tiger, the Panther, the Lynx, the Cat, the Seal, the Squirrel, the Rabbit, the Hare, the Chinchilli

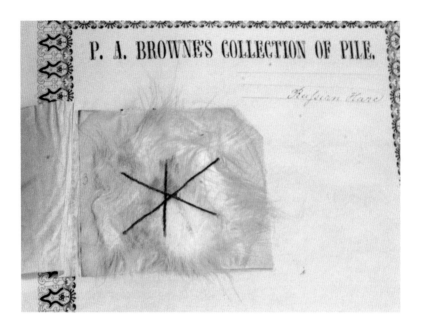

[*sic*], the Possum, the Kangaroo, the Stag, the Elk, the Antelope, the [wild] Sheep, [and] the [Mountain] Goat.[17]

Samples of all of these were in his collection at the time, and he planned to research and write about the relative merits of each of them.[18]

FROM ANIMAL TO HUMAN HAIR

It was not a big step for Browne to expand his study from quadrupedal to human hair. Through this he believed "the mooted question of the unity or plurality of races might easily be settled, and that of the crossing of species and formation of varieties readily explained."[19] With friendships he had established through his

P. A. BROWNE'S COLLECTION OF PILE.

Whiskers.

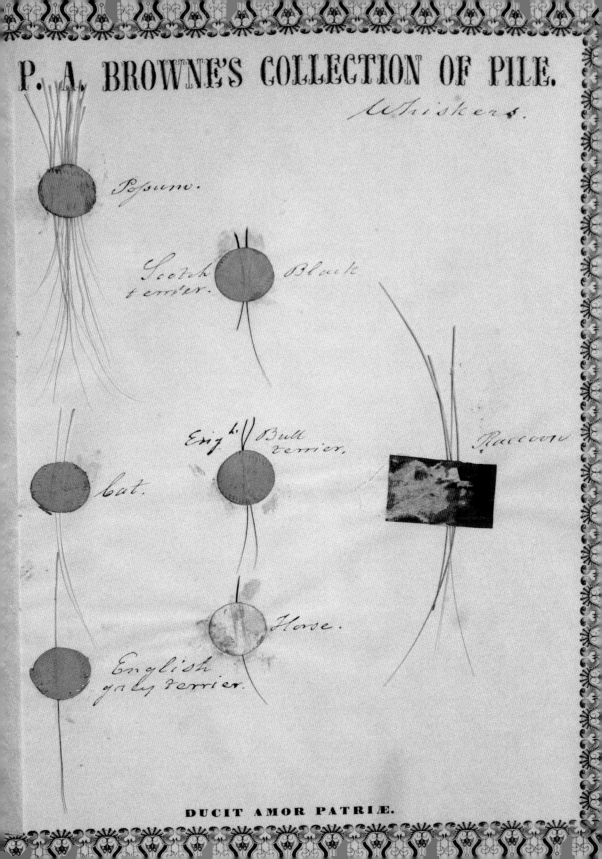

Possum.

Scotch terrier. Black.

Cat.

Eng.ʰ Bull terrier.

Raccoon

Horse.

English grey terrier.

DUCIT AMOR PATRIÆ.

legal practice and help from scientific organizations in Philadelphia, Washington, and abroad, Browne began to gather human hair samples from around the world.

When Lieutenant Charles Wilkes was chosen to lead the U.S. government's first exploratory expedition to the South Pacific in 1838, Browne asked him to collect animal fur and to obtain hair specimens from any indigenous people he might encounter. Wilkes graciously added Browne's charge to the many other scientific responsibilities mandated by Congress for the expedition. After six years of travel, from South America to Antarctica and Australia to the Pacific Northwest, he presented Browne with a bountiful supply of the fur and hair he had requested.[20]

While he waited for Wilkes's extended expedition to return, Browne sought other hair samples with the help of a growing network of doctors, soldiers, and government agents throughout the United States and in western territories not yet part of the Union. He made a special effort to collect the locks of Native Americans and to classify each sample by the tribal affiliation of its source. He also tried to comprehend the implications of crossbreeding among unrelated groups, requesting hair from people of mixed backgrounds often overlooked or ignored by the social historians of his time. In addition, he wished to obtain hair "from persons laboring under diseases of the hair or diseases of the skin likely to affect the hair."[21]

The hair samples he received were both cut and pulled, to include their roots and follicles.[22] These were tied in small bundles with silk ribbons or string, fixed to the decorated pages of his albums, and captioned with whatever documentation he had and with "the particulars that render it curious."[23]

P. A. BROWNE'S COLLECTION OF PILE.

A "Peguan Talain" living
at Rangoon, Burman
Empire. See No. 1.

N. B. McCulloch says
that the Burmese have
coarse lank hair with
olive complexions.

Taken from a Peguan Talain
born at Rangoon 29 years ago
A Male recently come over to
Siam

DUCIT AMOR PATRIÆ.

P. A. BROWNE'S COLLECTION OF PILE.

Noah Webster L.L.D.

DUCIT AMOR PATRIÆ.

CELEBRITY HAIR

It was perhaps inevitable that a person interested in studying the "locks of hair or wool of the heads of persons of all nations, races, sects, and varieties" would eventually find a more manageable subset of his subject to study in detail.[24] Like other naturalists of his day, Browne decided to look for similarities and differences between the mass of humanity and exceptional figures who had attained unusual levels of distinction in society. Even as he continued to make generic pleas for hair samples through his wide network of correspondents, he began to make more targeted, personal requests: James Fenimore Cooper, Noah Webster, Henry Clay, Jefferson Davis, and Charles Willson Peale were among the celebrities, dead and alive, whose locks he was eager to obtain, preserve, and study.[25] The public figures he sought out were most often male, but in his public solicitations he made clear that he was interested in obtaining "locks of hair of distinguished persons, whether male or female, and either at home or abroad." These, he promised, would be "carefully preserved in a distinct cabinet."[26]

Browne's reputation as a scientist and the cogent explanations he was able to give in his requests elicited almost uniformly positive responses from those to whom he wrote. If a historical figure whose hair he wanted was no longer living, he would contact that person's family, knowing that next of kin almost always retained such keepsakes. Thus Browne was able to add hair samples from George Washington, Thomas Jefferson, John Adams, and several signers of the Declaration of Independence to his "cabinet." Each such sample bolstered the credibility of his effort and made the next request easier to fulfill.[27]

Most of the letters that accompany the samples reflect the seriousness with which Browne's correspondents took his requests. Happy to contribute to what they recognized as a worthy field of research, some voluntarily included the hair of important friends and relatives. James Buchanan wrote an apology to Browne in 1849 because his hair had been recently cut and so he could not provide it when asked. A few months later he wrote a second letter enclosing the requested lock.[28]

Not all of Browne's celebrity exchanges were as cordial. One instance, for which both sides of the correspondence still exist, demonstrates just how imperious, persistent—even rude—Peter Browne could be in his single-minded drive to complete his presidential hair collection. In a letter of September 1853 the recently retired president Millard Fillmore responded to Peter Browne's request and agreed to supply a sample of his hair. He neglected, however, to enclose it with his letter. Browne interpreted the oversight as a failure to observe "the common rules of courtesy which regulate the intercourse of gentlemen" and as a personal insult. "You must admit," he chided Fillmore in a scathing reply,

> that it would have been an honor conferred upon you to have [your lock of hair] placed, as I intended, along side of those of Washington, Jefferson, Adams, Tyler, etc, etc. . . . I attribute your default [in not sending the requested sample] to deficiency in your early education.[29]

Benj Franklin one of the Signers of the Dec of Indep

Doctor Franklin

Mrs Duane regrets that it
is not in her power to comply
with Mr Browne's request she
has no hair of her Grandfather,
but remembers to have seen a
lock in possession of her Father,
which was bequeathed to a Brother,
she will make enquiries about it
of his daughters, and if possible
procure a portion of it for Mr B—

Wednesday Nov 29 /48

Browne's clash with President Fillmore was the exception rather than the rule, however; he generally achieved positive results in his quest. Throughout the 1840s and '50s he enlisted explorers, missionaries, and traders of foreign goods to send him hair samples from the heads of people they met or worked with in Africa, Asia, North and South America, Australasia, Oceania, and the High Arctic.[30] From Washington, D.C., Alexander H. H. Stuart, Millard Fillmore's secretary of the interior, forwarded Browne's requests to agents in the Bureau of Indian Affairs, who in turn responded with a wide array of specimens from Native Americans.

Joseph Henry, the first secretary of the Smithsonian Institution, was especially helpful in gathering material. He offered to forward Browne's solicitation letters for both animal and human hair to all parts of the world. "We are in direct correspondence with about five hundred institutions and [with] three hundred men of science abroad," he wrote. "To all these a copy [of Browne's solicitation] might be forwarded if thought desirable."[31]

When Browne sought Henry's advice about what to do with his collection, Henry replied that he would be happy to have it come to the Smithsonian, but he recommended first offering it to either the American Philosophical Society, the Academy of Natural Sciences of Philadelphia, or the Natural History Society of Boston, to best serve the academic community. "I mention these institutions in preference to the Smithsonian," he wrote, "because the number of persons who would be interested in the subject would be greater in either Philadelphia or Boston than in Washington." At the Academy in Philadelphia, Henry advised, the collection would be "carefully preserved and at the same time

P. R. Browne's Collection of Pile.

sent by Mr Fletcher.

Scalp of a Sioux
Warrior taken by the
Patager Indians.

58.

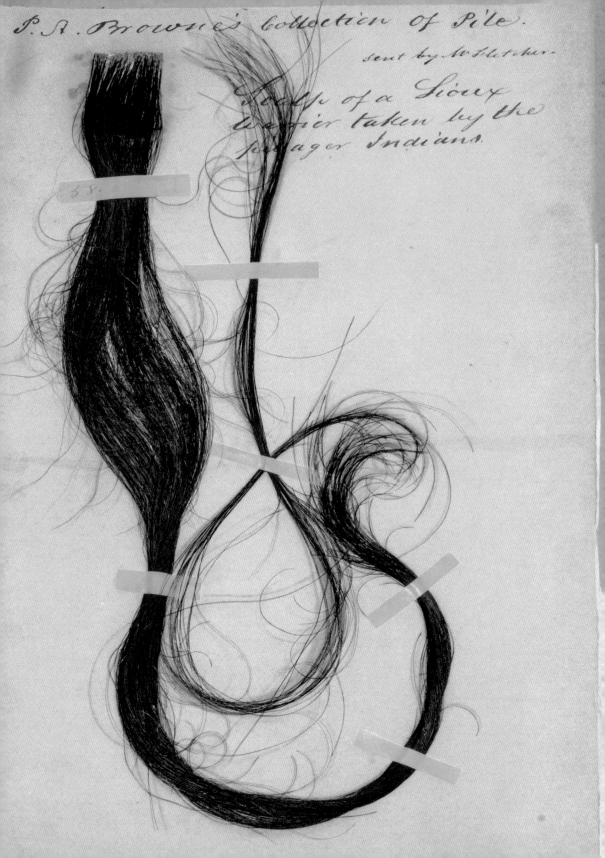

P. A. BROWNE'S COLLECTION OF PILE.

Umbadula, aged bet. 18 & 20, mule, Amagengoma Tribe.

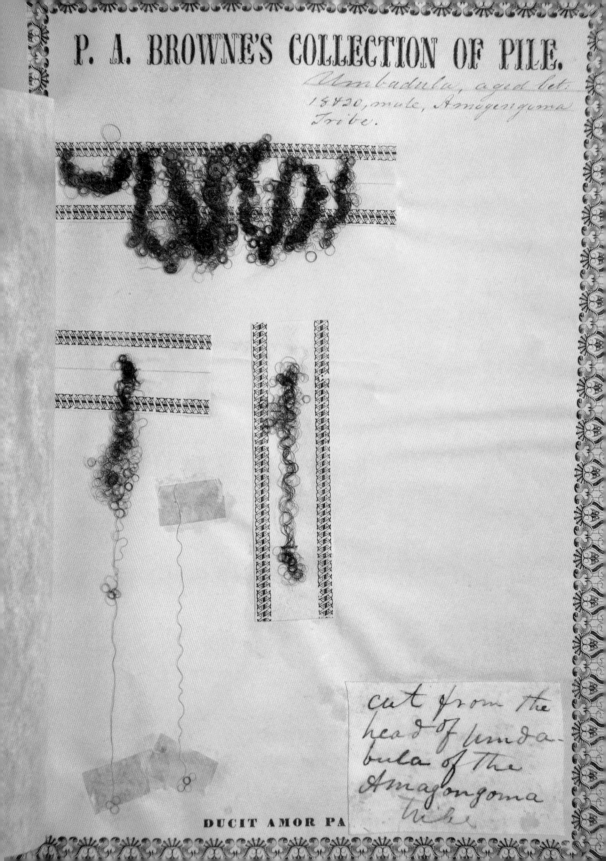

cut from the head of Umdabula of the Amagongoma Tribe.

DUCIT AMOR PA

rendered accessible for reference and study to any person who may hereafter be engaged in this line of investigation."[32] And so it has been.

When Browne died in 1860, his collection had become, as far as we know, the largest of its kind in the world.[33] He died convinced that much more research was needed in this promising field. South Pacific fishermen, Inuit seal hunters, slaves from Africa, politicians, war heroes, artists, writers, a "Hungarian patriot," a convicted murderer (whose hair samples Browne collected before and after his hanging), the Dauphin of France, and Napoleon Bonaparte were among the hundreds of people represented in his collection.[34]

FROM SAINTLY TO POLITICAL

In Western culture samples of human hair have long been sought and preserved as relics of religious, political, and personal significance. The Catholic Church, from the time of its founding, has made a special effort to preserve the tangible remains of its most inspirational leaders.[35] A brisk trade in the hair and body parts of religious figures took place throughout the Middle Ages and well into the Renaissance. Hair samples from saints of both genders were among the most highly cherished relics in many European churches throughout these periods.[36] Sometimes these sacred objects were preserved in jewel-emblazoned reliquaries or in portable altars, which, when properly blessed, became consecrated spaces in themselves. One such altar made in Germany between 1190 and 1200 and now in the British Museum contains the relics of forty saints, including hair attributed to Saint John the Evangelist.[37] Moved from place to place for religious ceremonies, this

Albrecht Dürer, detail, *Self-Portrait at Twenty-Eight*, 1500

portable altar and others like it brought holy artifacts to those unable to travel to churches or sacred sites where relics were permanently housed.[38]

Even when dismemberment of corpses fell out of favor and saintly parts became hard to find, the collecting of hair samples continued to be an acceptable way to preserve not only religious figures but other significant people who have shaped the world, from Ludwig van Beethoven to Amelia Earhart, from Charlemagne to John Wilkes Booth.[39] Some of these remain in private hands; others are in institutions. The hair of the German Renaissance artist Albrecht Dürer, reportedly snipped from his head two days after his death in 1528 and sent to Strasbourg to his former pupil Hans Baldung, was deposited in 1873 in the Academy of Art in Vienna, where it is kept in a silver reliquary. Other figures whose locks are owned by academic institutions include William Shakespeare (Folger Library), Lord Byron (University of Delaware), Henry Wadsworth Longfellow (Historical Society of Maine), and John Keats (Houghton Library at Harvard). The hair of the nineteenth-century Hungarian composer Franz Liszt, the English poet Robert Browning, and

Lock of Nathaniel Hawthorne's hair, Isabella Stewart Gardner Museum

the American novelist Nathaniel Hawthorne are among the fibrous relics housed at the Isabella Stewart Gardner Museum in Boston.[40]

Mixing science and politics, Dominique Vivant Denon, the director of the Louvre and other French museums under Napoleon, made a reliquary that included the beard of Henry IV, a tooth of Voltaire, and a lock of Napoleon's hair, donated by the Emperor himself.[41] When Captain James Cook was killed by natives in Hawaii, a clump of hair was taken from his battered head, placed in a coffin-shaped, silver-decorated wooden box, and given to the explorer's wife. It is today at the State Library of New South Wales in Sydney, Australia, along with an envelope containing hair of the explorer Robert O'Hara Burke, who perished from heat, thirst, and starvation in 1861 while attempting the first crossing of Australia from south to north—a distance of some 2,000 miles—with his partner William John Wills, who likewise perished.[42]

An increased popularity of hair collecting, both public and private, happened to coincide with the time when Peter Browne launched his scientific study. This no doubt helped him in his quest for the hair of national and international celebrities.

GEORGE WASHINGTON'S HAIR

For its patriotic significance, Browne considered the hair of George Washington the jewel in the crown of his collection. Represented with almost as many hair samples as portraits and autographs in museum collections, George Washington is a good case study in the popularity of celebrity hair collecting.[43] Immediately after the president's death and for most of the century that followed, Americans turned to shrines and relics to remind themselves of their hero's greatness. Just as Europeans had done with saints in the Middle Ages, the American public craved physical proof of the reality of their fallen leader. Patriotic Americans clipped Washington's signature from his letters and other documents. Some made crosses and other souvenirs from his wooden coffin when it was exhumed and replaced with marble in 1831. But the most ubiquitous of Washington's relics are the locks of his hair that were enclosed in brooches, rings, pins, and framed displays. They are today found in libraries, museums, historical societies, and private collections across the country. The hair sample in Peter Browne's collection is but one of hundreds attributed to the nation's founding father.

Until they began to change hands commercially in the twentieth century, most examples of Washington's hair could be traced by descent from someone who had received clippings directly from the president and first lady or from Tobias Lear,

Washington's secretary and aide, who was assigned the job of distributing presidential relics to friends and admirers after Washington's death. In his detailed account of Washington's burial, Lear described cutting off some of the president's hair just after his body was placed in its coffin.[44] He may have been collecting a memento for himself, but more likely he was laying in a supply of hair for the barrage of requests he knew he and the Washington family would soon receive.

Another logical, if slightly less reliable, source of Washington's hair was Martin Pierie, the barber who groomed the president in Philadelphia. According to his son John, during the 1780s the elder Pierie snipped and kept a good supply of the president's famous hair. When the younger Pierie followed in his father's barbering footsteps, he used the trove of presidential pile handed down to him to curry favor or advertise his own hair-cutting services. It was John Pierie who gave Browne the Washington sample that Browne so prized.[45] Browne added this specimen to his cabinet for scientific study, but other Washington hair samples, dispensed during Washington's lifetime and afterward, were kept as memento mori or used for personal adornment by their owners.[46]

Families in the nineteenth century whose American ancestry predated the Revolution took great pride in their national heritage. Descendants of those who had fought in the War for Independence or who had known Washington personally felt a special status. Wearing cuff links, a brooch, locket, or ring with a few strands from the first president demonstrated a close connection to the nation's birth and its founding father.

The Washingtons had embraced the practice common among well-to-do families in the eighteenth century of displaying hair from a friend or loved one. Martha Washington was said to have always worn a locket that "almost invariably . . . contained a miniature of her husband, generally with a lock of his hair set in the back, to which she attached a great deal of sentiment."[47] The Washingtons did not keep all such mementos to themselves. As early as 1770 George Washington sent strands of his hair overseas to have them put into lockets that throughout their lives he and Martha gave to their family and friends.[48]

Mourning pin with braided hair of George and Martha Washington, Winterthur Museum, Delaware

HAIR AND HUMANITY

The collection and trading of hair in the eighteenth and nineteenth centuries wasn't limited to luminaries such as Washington. Hair was a common gift between friends and relatives as a token of their love. "Friendship albums" or "valentine albums" often included woven-hair rings and hearts and ribboned tufts of hair, along with poems and loving inscriptions from their donors. Albums with hair from friends and relatives were especially popular among young girls.

Men, too, were sentimental collectors of hair. Missing his wife, Lucy, while he was in Edinburgh in 1826, the American artist and naturalist John James Audubon wrote home to ask her to "send me by first opportunity as much of thy hair as will make me a cord for my watch."[49] Napoleon Bonaparte had a similar watch cord made from his hair to be given to his son after his death.[50] Hair conveyed remembrance too for the poet Emily Dickinson, who sent a friend a snippet of her hair "to

Lock of Emily Dickinson's hair,
Amherst College Archives and Special Collections

make you remember me when [my] locks are crisp and gray."
She wrote, "I shall never give you anything again that will be
half so full of sunshine as this wee lock of hair, but I wish no hue
more somber might ever fall to you."[51]

Hair remained deeply symbolic throughout the nineteenth
century whether it was simply mailed to a friend or incorporated in mourning jewelry, a form of personal adornment
made especially popular by Queen Victoria after the death of
her husband in 1861. Shadow boxes with intricate wreaths,
hearts, and crosses woven from hair were seen in many Vic-
torian homes on both sides of the Atlantic, as were glass bell
jars filled with bouquets of "flowers" made from the hair of
family members and friends.[52] As the popularity of these grew,
the demand for human hair to create such displays exceeded
the locally grown supply. In 1859 some 150,000 to 200,000
pounds of human hair were imported to the United States. By
1875 three times that amount was being imported to augment

the personal hair used in the primary focus of the compositions.[53] At midcentury the money generated by the import of human hair stood between $800,000, and $1 million per year, with prices ranging from $15 to $200 per pound, depending on its hue, length, and texture.[54]

Peter Browne undoubtedly saw many examples of mourning jewelry and artfully arranged hair displays in the homes of his friends and understood the deep emotional meaning they held for their owners. But his motivation to collect hair was far from such sentiment; it was the apex of his lifelong quest to understand the diversity of life.

For his studies Browne sought well documented specimens from as wide a range of sources as possible. He wished to know from whom each hair sample had come, when the hair was collected, how old its donor was, and any information about the person's genealogy. For the background on specimens from far-flung places, Browne relied on data from either the donors themselves or the intermediaries who served as his collectors.

His friends and donors were consistently positive in their support of his efforts. "The subject to which you have paid so much attention is one intimately connected with the natural history of man, and has undoubtedly an important bearing on some of the philosophical points which are now under discussion by the scientific world," wrote Joseph Henry in 1858.[55] "When our remains shall be mouldering in their graves, your useful labors will be felt and understood," wrote another of Browne's correspondents, reflecting on the timelessness of the hair specimen he was sending.[56]

P. A. BROWNE'S COLLECTION OF PILE.

Dr Sir   Phila Jany 29 1849

In compliance with my promise to you
I enclose you two small locks of hair, the first
opportunity I have had.   I hope your
philosophical researches on the subject may
gratify yourself & prove to us that there
are more things in Heaven & Earth than
are now dreamt of in our philosophy

Yr Svt
Tho: Sergeant

P. A. Browne Esq

THE VAST REACH OF BROWNE'S COLLECTION

Browne's worldwide collection of hair enabled him to compare people of different ethnographic backgrounds and document the development of humans at different ages, from their start in the womb ("piles of the foetus in all the stages of gestation"), to the

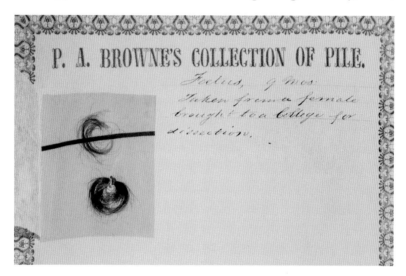

end of their lives, or even beyond ("hair grown after death").[57] As he approached his own death, he saved a snip of his own hair at age seventy-three. And he was pleased to include in his collection a sample from a hundred-year-old man and another from one who claimed to be 120.[58]

Ultimately, Browne's studies represented every facet of the human condition. He obtained examples of hair from the insane: patients at the Pennsylvania Hospital, the Western Virginia Lunatic Asylum, and the Ohio Lunatic Asylum. He received specimens from the Otoe [Otto] and Omaha [Indian] Mission School and the

Medical College of Charleston. He also sought and successfully obtained hair from people who were deaf and mute and from the sightless patients at the Perkins Institute, the first "asylum" or school for the blind in the United States, established in 1829.

In an album marked "Pile of Remarkable Persons," Browne preserved the hair of Julia Pastrana, a bearded lady dubbed "The Misnomered Bear Woman";[59] "Black Hawk, Chief of the Menominees";[60] "Rob Hales, the English Quaker Giant"; "the Liliputian King"; and the famous "Siamese twins" Chang and Eng Bunker.[61] He also had several examples of albino hair, a sample of hair that had "turned grey in one night from fright," and the hair "of the head of a lady which had laid 32 years in the grave."[62]

Also in his collection and cited in his publications are hair samples from Egyptian mummies given to him by the man credited with introducing Egyptology to North America, George R. Gliddon, the U.S. vice consul to Egypt from 1832 to 1840. After living in Egypt for almost two decades, Gliddon became well known in the United States by traveling throughout the country displaying a moving panorama of the Nile River. He gave live performances in which he presented captivating stories of life in ancient Egypt. Standing onstage between two large tables, one piled high with copies of the chief works on Egyptology, the other with relics of Egypt, Gliddon lectured to rapt audiences while the panorama of majestic scenes of ancient Egypt moved slowly along the walls and soft strains of oriental music filled the hall.[63] The effect was mesmerizing. "Once placed within a hall thus adorned," wrote one enchanted viewer, "the visitor found himself in a new and magic region; the present vanished, and

P. A. BROWNE'S COLLECTION OF PILE.

Hair of the "Liliputian King"
exhibited in Philad.ª in 1853/4
He is 16 inches high, — nearly
4 years old, & weighs 6 ℔ 4 oz

DUCIT AMOR PATRIÆ.

the men and the events of thirty and forty centuries back arose before his gaze."[64]

Peter Browne had been among Gliddon's audiences, which ranged from a few hundred to several thousand people and averaged five hundred per performance. It is estimated that by 1849 more than 100,000 people had heard Gliddon speak.[65] Gliddon's popular publications further spread the story of Egypt's ancient past. His books sold in large numbers, and one of his articles, published as an "extra" in Park Benjamin's *New World* magazine, went through twelve editions, selling some 24,000 copies within five years.[66]

Browne was impressed by Gliddon's accounts of ancient life and was pleased to receive Egyptian hair samples from him, but he kept a careful distance from the diplomat turned showman. A complicated and at times contradictory figure, Gliddon was described by one historian as "a name-dropper, a sponger, a swinger on the shirttails of the great, a braggart, pretender, and scatologist." He went on:

> Gliddon was also courageous, generous, warm-hearted and loyal, and a friend worth having. The pendulum of his frenetic personality constantly swung between boundless joy and utter despair. Proclaiming himself the eternal and implacable foe of humbug, he was himself a master of the art of puffing. Hopelessly addicted to the polysyllable and relishing the ponderosities of Victorian prose, he never blighted with boredom the life of anyone.[67]

Mathew B. Brady. Daguerreotype of
George Robbins Gliddon, 1853–54

Browne compared the mummy hair Gliddon sent to him with that of mummies from Peru, Mexico, and Brazil given to him by the more reserved physical anthropologist Samuel George Morton, who collected and studied human skulls during the height of the nineteenth-century polygenesis-monogenesis debate and was probably the one who introduced Browne to Gliddon.[68] Browne incorporated the ancient hair into his global survey of contemporary pile, attempting to understand patterns of human distribution and the relationships between groups that they reveal.

CLASSIFYING HAIR

Browne summarized his findings in a paper he sent to the Academy of Natural Sciences of Philadelphia in 1851. In it Browne stated that "the hair of the head of man [is] of three principal shapes, viz.: 1. The cylindrical; 2. The oval; and 3. The eccentrically elliptical. Of the first [group] I have noticed the ancient hairs from Peru, Mexico, Brazil, &c., those of our present Indians and the Chinese. Of the second, the hairs of the English, French, Hungarians, Germans and Americans, &c., &c. And of the third, the wool of the Bushman and African negro."[69]

He reconfirmed his three-part division of hair types in an 1852 publication entitled *Classification of Mankind by the Hair*

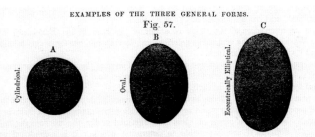

Fig. 57.

Of the Particular Forms.—But there are other shapes, less frequently met with, viz: the cylin*droidal*, the lesser ov*oidal*, the greater ov*oidal*, and the eccentrically ellip*toidal*, to which we give the name of " the *particular* forms of pile."

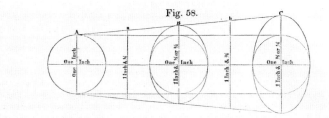

Fig. 58.

The three forms of hair identified in Browne's *Trichologia Mammalium*

and Wool of Their Heads. The following year, he took his findings a step further by equating different hair types with the different origins of the people who grew them. "There are three distinct species of human beings inhabiting this globe," he declared in *Trichologia Mammalium*. And so it had been, he asserted, citing his mummy research, "for at least from 2,700 to 3,000 years—probably from the first creation of man."[70]

Browne's assessment of hair shape, thickness, and strength may have been accurate, but his conclusion that this was evidence of man's division into three separate species was not. He further undermined the validity of his thinking by sorting the different hair types he had discovered into a qualitative order. "The hair of the white man is more perfect than that of the negro," he wrote.[71]

Not surprisingly, Brown's assertions were seized upon by people eager for any scientific support for the racially biased social, economic, and political order of the day. The polygenists, who believed that humankind evolved from two or more distinct—and decidedly unequal—species, were delighted to learn that hair could be used to support their conviction that the white Caucasian male stood at the pinnacle of a hierarchical pyramid.[72] In the pre–Civil War American South, where slavery was still far from outlawed, Peter Browne's research on hair thus helped to reinforce what the supporters of slavery wanted to believe.[73]

Browne acknowledged the "numerous disappointments and . . . many difficulties arising out of ignorance and prejudice" he had encountered in his study of hair.[74] "In a path so little trodden," he wrote, "it is to be expected that we should occasionally make mis-steps; but we trust that all such will be attributed to inadvertence."[75] He assured his readers that if and when further evidence was acquired, he would gladly correct any mistakes he might have made.[76]

Unfortunately, Browne did not live long enough to rethink his conclusion about hair structure as a determining factor in human speciation or witness the damaging effect his ideas would have on the racially charged political debates leading to the American Civil War. Nor did he have the opportunity to apply Charles Darwin's theories about evolution to his investigations, for Darwin's book *On the Origin of Species* was published just months before Browne's death, and his *Descent of Man* was not

P. A. BROWNE'S COLLECTION OF PILE.

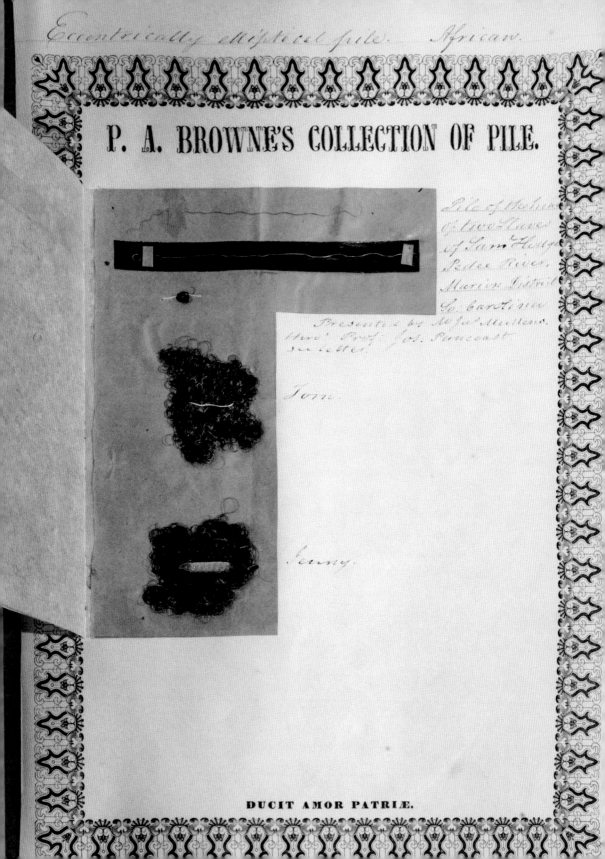

Pile of the hair
of two Slaves
of Sam Hodge
Pedee River,
Marien District
So. Carolina.

Presented by Mr Jas Mullens.
thro' Prof. Jos. Pancoast
in a letter.

Tom.

Jenny.

DUCIT AMOR PATRIÆ.

published until 1871. Although they knew and corresponded with some of the same people, there is no correspondence between Browne and Darwin and no evidence that they ever had any direct communication.

THE VALUE OF PRESERVATION

Since Peter Browne began amassing his national collection in the 1840s, the science of hair analysis has come a long way. Hair is now recognized as an important source for clues to a wide range of historical questions. It was key in proving Thomas Jefferson's intimate relationship with Sally Hemings, and samples of Napoleon Bonaparte's hair in European collections were analyzed to try to determine if Napoleon was poisoned during his exile on St. Helena.[77] In recent years historians using the DNA extracted from samples of ancient human hair have pushed back, by tens of thousands of years, earlier assumptions about the timing and direction of human migrations.

"A lock of hair, collected by a British anthropologist a century ago, has yielded the first genome of an Australian Aborigine," wrote Nicholas Wade in the *New York Times* in September 2011.[78] Wade's article reported that a team of scientists at the Natural History Museum of Denmark had revealed that Australia's native people had come "from the ancestral human homeland somewhere in northeast Africa."[79] The scientists' findings bolstered earlier genetic evidence that "once the Aborigines' ancestors arrived in Australia, some 50,000 years ago, they managed to keep the continent to themselves without admitting outsiders."[80] Wade quoted Dr. Eske Willerslev, director of the Center for Geo-Genetics at the University of Copenhagen, who concluded that

"The Aborigines are thus direct descendants of the first modern humans to leave Africa, without any genetic mixture from other races, so far as can be seen at present." Use of the older hair was critical to the research, Wade explained, because it "reduced the possibility of mixture with European genes, and sidestepped the political difficulties of obtaining DNA from living Aborigines."[81]

Human hair was also critical to Dr. Willerslev and his colleagues in tracking the origins of Paleo-Eskimo culture in Western Greenland.[82] Summarizing a paper published in the science journal *Nature* in 2010, Faye Flam reported in the *Philadelphia Inquirer* that, based on "nothing but a few hairs left in the tundra," Willerslev had conducted a DNA analysis that filled in "gaps in the story of the peopling of the Americas" with dramatic new information. This study, "the first such genetic sequencing of an ancient human," revealed a 4,000-year-old "dark-skinned, brown-eyed young male [whose] people, known as the Saqqaq, branched off from the Siberians some 5,500 years ago," beginning an early trek across the Bering Strait. "The findings," Flam wrote, "reinforce the idea that people came from Asia to the Americas in waves. The finding also illustrates how fast scientists are advancing in their ability to decipher DNA—and how much could be learned about any of us from a hair."[83]

There's no question of the faults of interpretation made by Browne and other influential men of science, such as the Harvard biologist Louis Agassiz in the mid-nineteenth century. As Flam wrote in 2016, "From his travels around the world, Darwin realized that there was no scientific reason to divide people into four races." And yet, "even after Darwin published his book,

Agassiz continued to promote the notion that Africans and Europeans were different species."[84]

Even though one of Browne's reasons for assembling his collection may have been to contribute to the now discredited study of race theory ("perhaps the worst idea ever to come out of science," suggests Flam), Browne's pile samples are still objects of enormous historical value. The analytical techniques of today are far beyond what Peter Browne could have dreamed of, and the hundreds of hair, fleece, and wool samples he so diligently gathered have resurfaced as invaluable tools in the modern search for knowledge about our past.

Like other rare historical collections, Browne's assemblage of pile provides an important window into our past. It is also a collection of surprising beauty and enduring curiosity. Browne would surely be gratified to know that these delicate threads of human and animal life, still in the archives of the Academy of Natural Sciences of Philadelphia more than a century and a half after he assembled them, hold answers to questions he himself was unable to resolve—and to many questions we ourselves have only begun to ask.

Specimens
of
Pile.

Collected by P. A. Browne

Department Nº 2.

Pile of Lower Animals.

Animal and Botanical

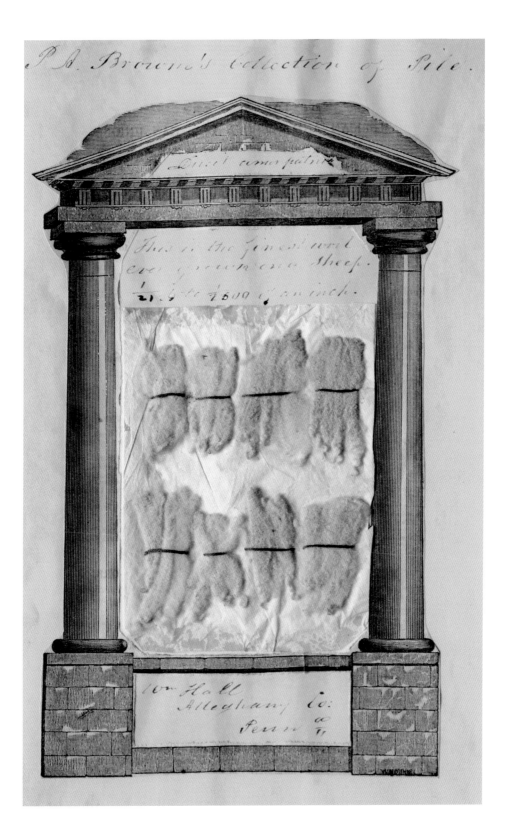

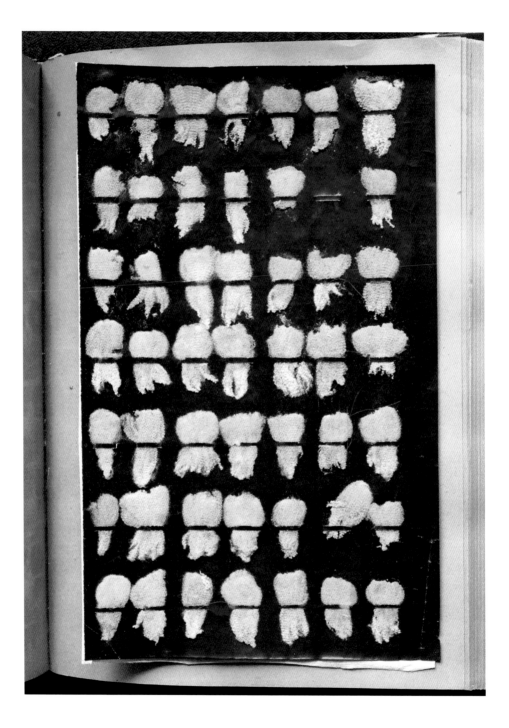

Angora Goat

Dr David' Ram 3 yr old exhibited at the Fair of the Penna State Ag' So: 1854 as a "Thibet Goat."

Description.

Head. forehead concave. Ears. of one buck & four ewes. broad. large & pendulous: - of others narrow. short & fox like. Note! The old lop-eared ewes drop kids with fox-ears. Lips. upper lip with slit or cut like the sheep. Teeth. same as sheep. Beard. all the males have beards & so have nearly all the females. The beard is shorter than in the common goat. Tegumentary appendage. Long. silky hair: no wool at the root. but the hair near the body is rather closer & thicker than on the outside. Tail. always carried erect. covered with bristling hairs. Foot. shape of the common goat. with that peculiar rasp-like rim which enables the animal to climb on rocks &c. Time of gestation. same as the common goat. Number of young. same as the sheep bring forth in June. Temper. gentle. Habit-quiet. Food - they combine browsing & grass eating. & incline towards the former. Are deep milkers.

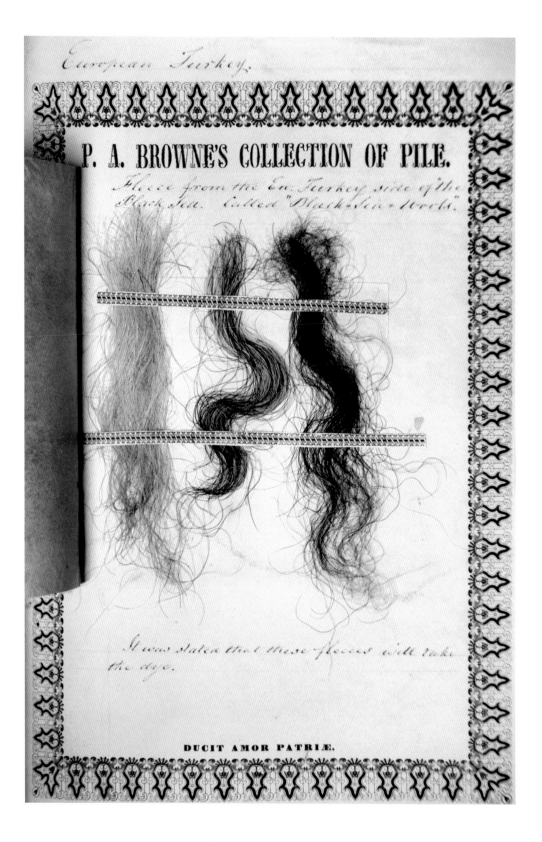

P. A. BROWNE'S COLLECTION OF PILE.

Fleece from the Eu: Turkey side of the
Black Sea. Called "Black=Sea=Wools".

It was stated that these fleeces will take
the dye.

DUCIT AMOR PATRIÆ.

United States

Georgia

P. A. BROWNE'S COLLECTION OF PILE.
Goat

1/4 Common or
3/4 Cashmere

1/4 Common Goat
3/4 Cashmere
a two crofses of the
Cashmere in the Common Go

DUCIT AMOR PATRIÆ.

A. BROWNE'S COLLECTION OF PILE.

Leo africanus

The Lion's mane

As exhibited at the Patent Transport.

DUCIT

THE LION.

DUCIT AMOR PATRIÆ.

Engraved by R. Sands. from a Drawing by R. Sands.

MALE AND FEMALE ELEPHANT, W

Tail.

P. A. BROWNE'S COLLECTION OF PILE.

Elephant.

Illustrations of Natural History

ER YOUNG ONE SUCKING.

P. A. BROWNE'S COLLECTION OF PILE.

Lutra canadensis

Mt. Rocky Mountains

THE OTTER.   THE SEA OTTER.

Mustela Lutra   *Mustela Lutris*

DUCIT AMOR PATRIÆ.

coleur artificial.

THE LYNX.

J. Le Keux sc.

R. Sands Jun. del.

DUCIT AMOR PATRIÆ.

The Silk of the
Silk Cotton Tree

Cotton

presented by Prof. J. K.
Mitchell.

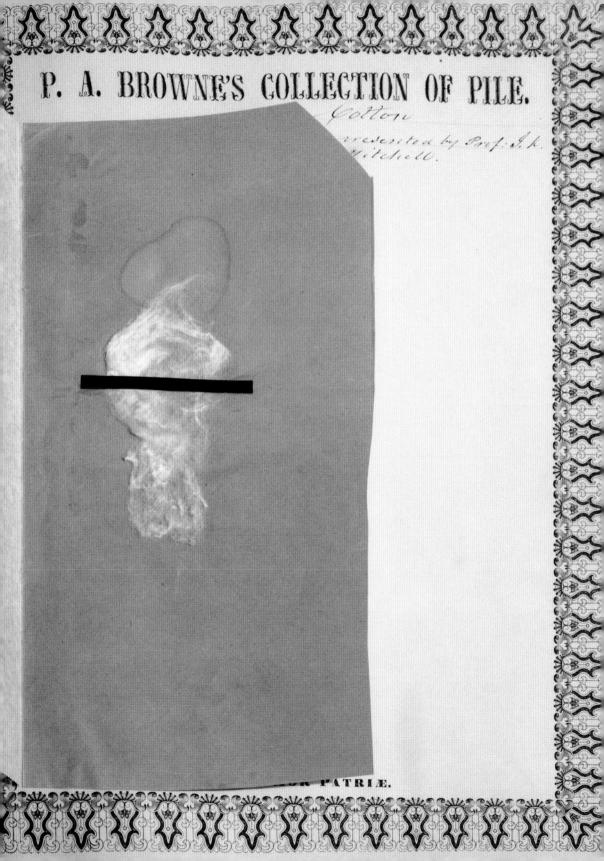

PATRIÆ.

Remarkable Persons

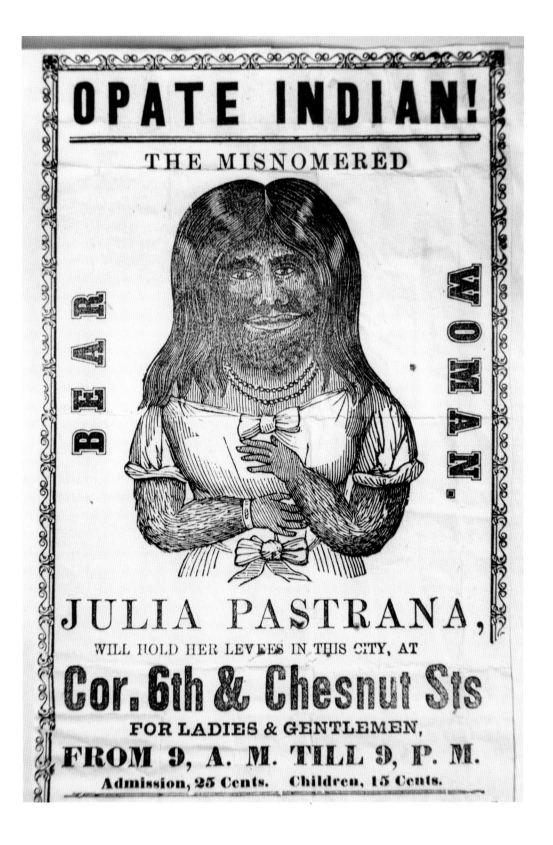

Julia Pastrana (1834–1860) was an indigenous woman born in the state of Sinaloa, Mexico, with congenital hypertrichosis terminalis (or generalized hypertrichosis lanuginosa). Her face and body were covered with straight black hair, her ears and nose were unusually large, and her teeth and jaw were irregular.

Performing as a singer and dancer from 1854 to 1860 before paying audiences in the United States and Europe, Pastrana became one of the most famous human curiosities of her time. In 1857 she married impresario Theodore Lent. Three years later, while in Moscow on tour, Pastrana died five days after a difficult childbirth to a boy who lived less than two days. Lent brought their bodies to a Russian anatomy professor who embalmed them, and Lent toured their corpses. "Unique in the annals of human exploitation," as the physician Jan Bondeson has covered in detail in his book *A Cabinet of Medical Curiosities* (1997), the corpses were exhibited for another 113 years. In February 2013, through the efforts of New York–based artist Laura Anderson Barbata, with the help of the Sinaloa state governor, the body of Julia Pastrana was turned over to the government of Sinaloa. (After a 1976 incident of vandalism the son's body was destroyed.) On February 12, 2013, hundreds of people attended her Catholic funeral and her remains were buried in a cemetery in Sinaloa de Leyva, a town near her birthplace.

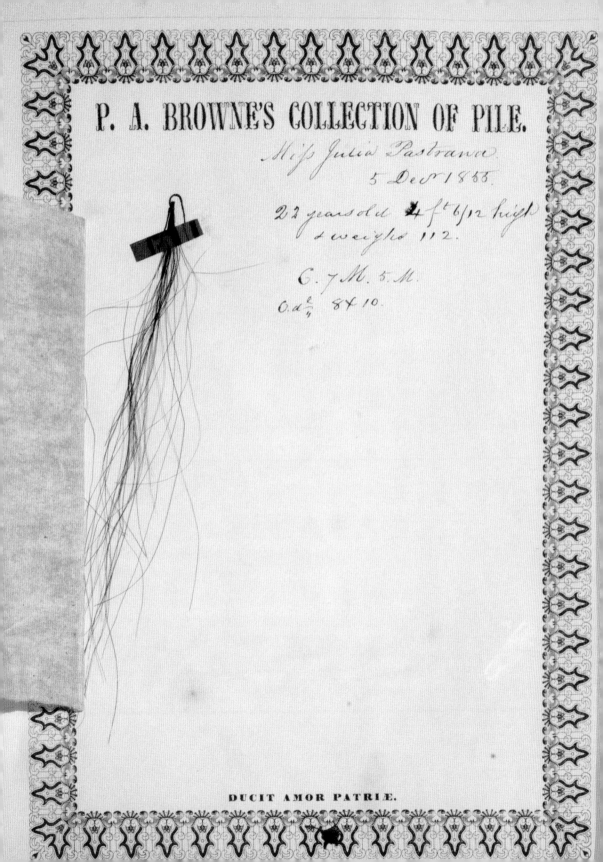

P. A. BROWNE'S COLLECTION OF PILE.

Miss Julia Pastrana.
5 Decr 1855.

22 years old 4 ft 6/12 high
& weighs 112.

C. 7 M. 5. M.
O. d.²⁄₄ 8 × 10.

DUCIT AMOR PATRIÆ.

Chang and Eng Bunker (1811–1874) were Thai-American conjoined twin brothers whose condition and birthplace became the basis for the term "Siamese twins." They were joined at the sternum by a small piece of cartilage, and their livers were fused. In 1829, Robert Hunter, a Scottish merchant who lived in Bangkok, saw the twins swimming and paid their parents to permit him to exhibit their sons as a curiosity on a world tour. When their contract with Hunter ended, Chang and Eng went into business for themselves and continued to tour for several years. In 1839, while visiting Wilkesboro, North Carolina, the brothers purchased a 110-acre farm in nearby Traphill. In 1843 Chang wed Adelaide Yates (1823–1917), while Eng married her sister, Sarah Anne (1822–1892). They maintained separate households, with a strict regimen of three days at one house and three at the other, and they had twenty-one children. Eng died approximately three hours after Chang; the doctor summoned to perform an emergency separation arrived too late.

P. A. BROWNE'S COLLECTION OF PILE.

The Siamese Twins

Cheong

1/325.

Eng.

1/355.

The Siamese Twins.

An exhibition of the Siamese Twins commenced in this city on Monday. The following account, derived from the Greensboro' (N. C.) Patriot, will prove interesting to the public:

Mr. Eng has six and Mr. Chang five children, all of whom are apt scholars and remarkably well be-haved. Messrs. Chang and Eng are alike remarkable for their industry and belligerent dispositions. They are strict and thorough-going business men, and woe to the unfortunate wight who dares to insult them. Formerly they resided in Wilkes county, but in consequence of the numerous actions for assault and battery brought against them in the county, they removed into the adjoining county, shortly after which they were fined $15 and costs at Rockport, the county seat, for splitting a board into splinters over the head of a man who had insulted them.

As regards the supposed sympathy exist-tween them, it may be stated that ....ing be-mate acquaintan... ..... their most int----ent of every thing of the kind, and give as in-s ances to sustain their opinion, that not long since they attended an auction sale of hogs, and bid against each other till they ran up the prices altogether above the market rates. Also, that on one occasion Mr. Eng or Chang was taken ill and took to his bed, where he lay complaining for some time, although his brother scolded him severely all the while for detaining him in bed, when he ought to have been attending to the business of their plantation. On another occasion, as they were passing up the road, a gentleman inquired of them where they were going —whereupon Mr. Eng replied, "I am going over the Blue Ridge, in the stage;" at the same instant Mr. Charg, looking over his shoulder, replied with an arch smile, "I am going back home to look after our wives and children." When questioned about their mother some time since by an acquaintance, they stated that they had formerly received letters from her, but latterly they had heard no tidings of her, and even if they were to receive letters from her written in the Siamese language, they would not be able to read them, as they had forgotten their mother tongue.

They are excellent hands to carry up a corner of a log house, exceeding all their neighbors in cutting saddles and notches in corner logs—both of them wielding the axe with a power and dexterity superior to any of the most expert woodcutters in this wooden country. When they chop or fight, they do so double-handed; and in driving a horse or chastising their negroes, both of them use the lash without mercy.

They are inveterate smokers and chewers of tobacco—each chewing his own quid and smoking his own pipe; it has been remarked, however, in support of the sympathy supposed to prevail through-out their systems, that as a general rule, when one takes a fresh quid, the other does the same. It is also generally admitted that there is a marked difference in the systems and temperaments of the gentle-men, but still they almost invariably draw the same inference from topics submitted to their considera-tion, and arrive at similar conclusions. Mr. Eng not unfrequently gives serious offence to Mr. Chang, by jesting him about his having one more child than he has. When shooting, (a sport they are very fond of,) one sights or takes aim, and the other, it is said, pulls the trigger; now if this be true, it would go far to prove the doctrine of supposed sympathy existing between the brothers, but it is questioned by most of the neighbors.

They readily admit and acknowledge themselves to entertain a strong christian faith or belief, and are regular attendants at church and other religious meetings, where they deport themselves as becomes good citizens of the land of their adoption. They are strong politicians, and take a lively interest in all elections that occur in their district. As the writer was informed by a lady of Mount Airy, "they are mighty stay at home people"—rarely ever going from home unless called away by business.

DUCIT AMOR PATRIÆ.

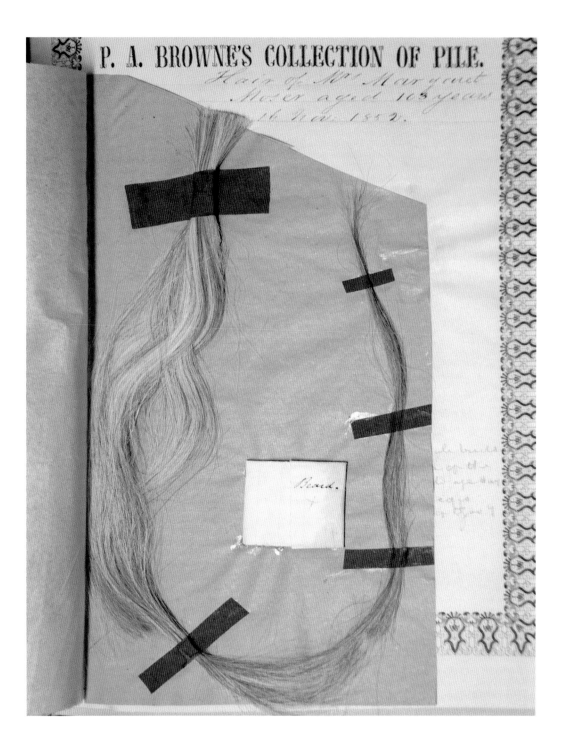

P. A. BROWNE'S COLLECTION OF PILE.

Hair of Mrs Margaret
Moser aged 103 years
16 Nov. 1852.

Beard.

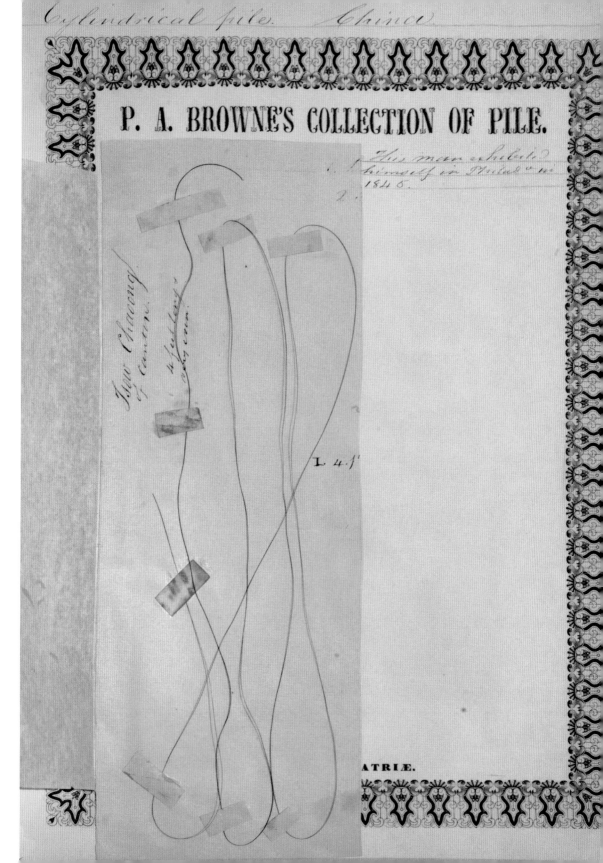

P. A. BROWNE'S COLLECTION OF PILE.

Turned grey in one night, from fright.

RIÆ.

Offset ghost image from an etching of the asylum in Browne's volume VII

The Ohio Lunatic Asylum

In 1838 construction by convict labor was completed and the state-supported Ohio Lunatic Asylum, located a mile from the capitol on 35 acres in Columbus, was opened. Under the direction of William Awl, MD, by 1850 it housed more than 300 patients, and in 1852 the state legislature agreed to build two more facilities. The building burned to the ground when a fire broke out one night in 1868. A new asylum was opened in 1877 in a Kirkbride building designed to house up to 800 patients. By 1935 it housed more than 2,900 patients. The building was demolished in the 1980s and early 1990s.

Ohio Lunatic Asylum
N. 25.

Male, aged 34, duration 15 y.
Dark hair & eyes, Dementia
Hereditary. Masturbation.

frosted.

94

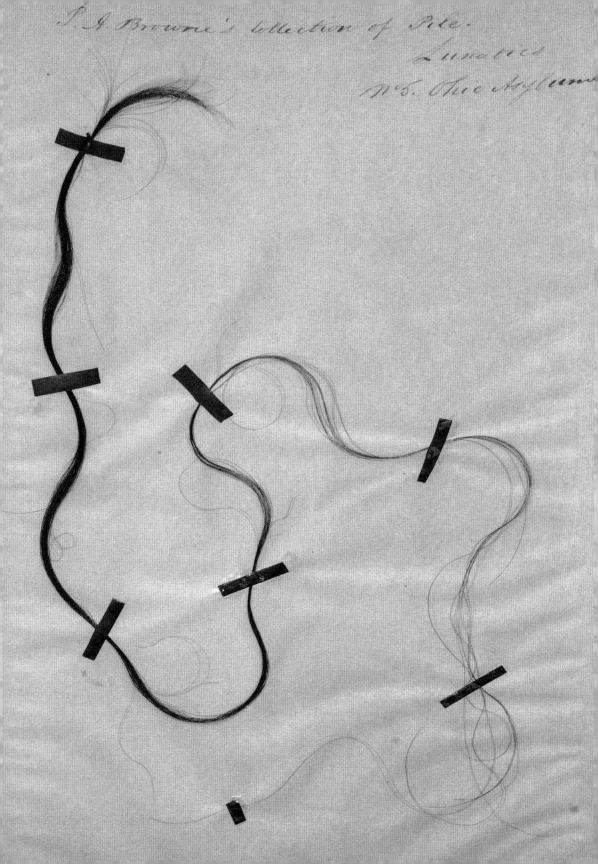

6

ay

523

5	10	3
5	2	3
6	2	3
6	6	3
7	3	3
7		3
8	2	3
8	3	3
8	4	3
8	5	0
8	6	3
8	7	3
		3
	8	3
9		3
		3
9	5	3
		3
	5	3
10	1	3
10	2	3

823

$\frac{1}{90}$

ay

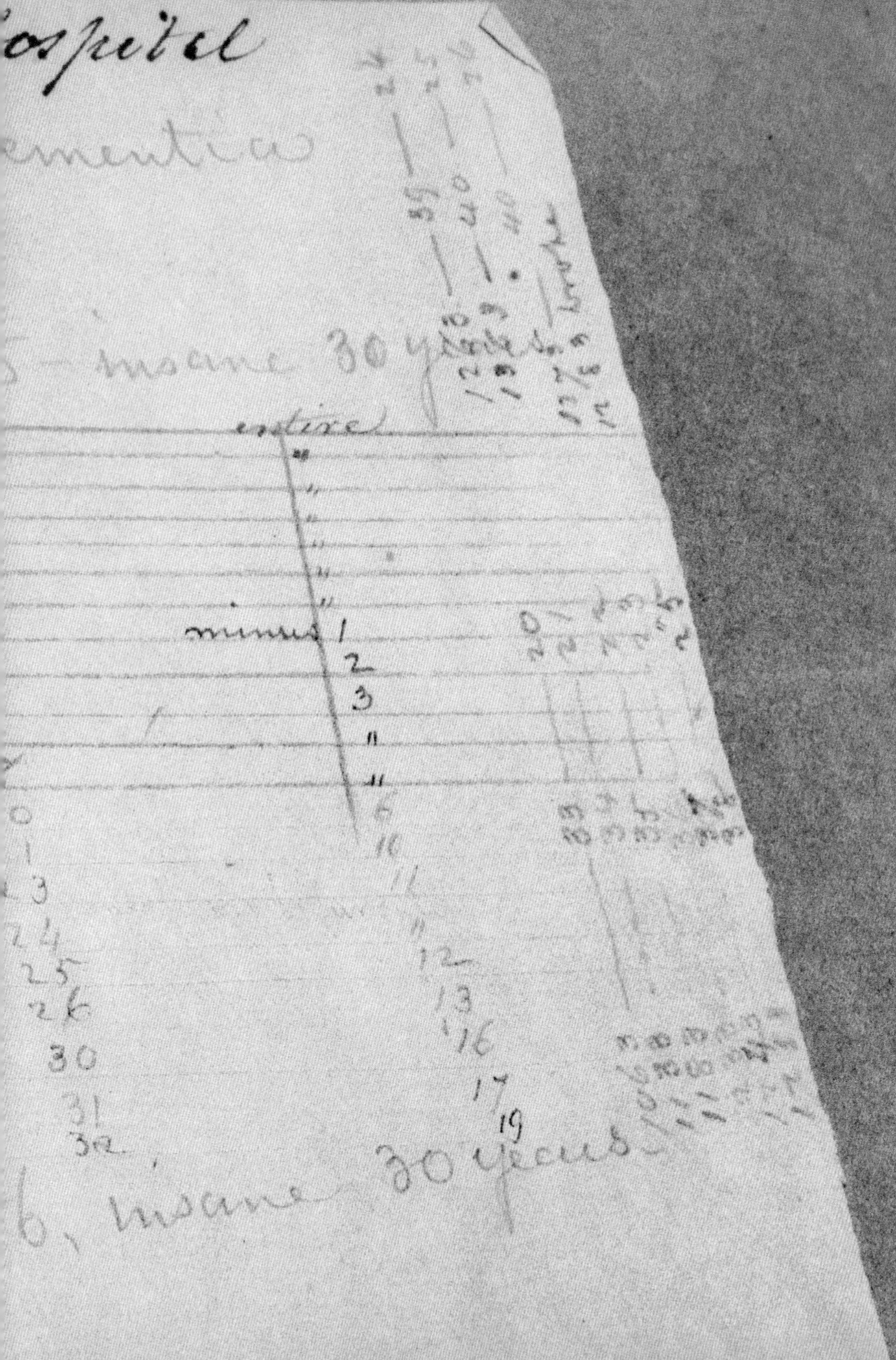

ospital

ementia

5 — insane 30 years

entirel

minus 1
2
3
"
"
6
10
11
"
12
13
16
17
19

0
3
24
25
26
30
31
32

6, insane 30 years

Presidents and Other Distinguished People

"Fame spread her wings and with her trumpet blew,
Great WASHINGTON is come, what praise is due—
What titles shall he have? She paus'd and said,
Not one—his *name alone* strikes every title dead."

His Excellency
John Adams.
President of the U.S.

Panicum.

This grew upon the Grave
of Thos Jefferson.
1826.

His Excellency
Thomas Jefferson
President of the U.S.

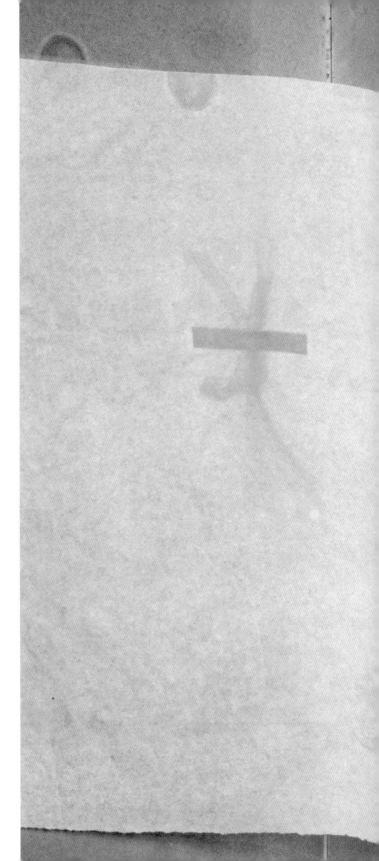

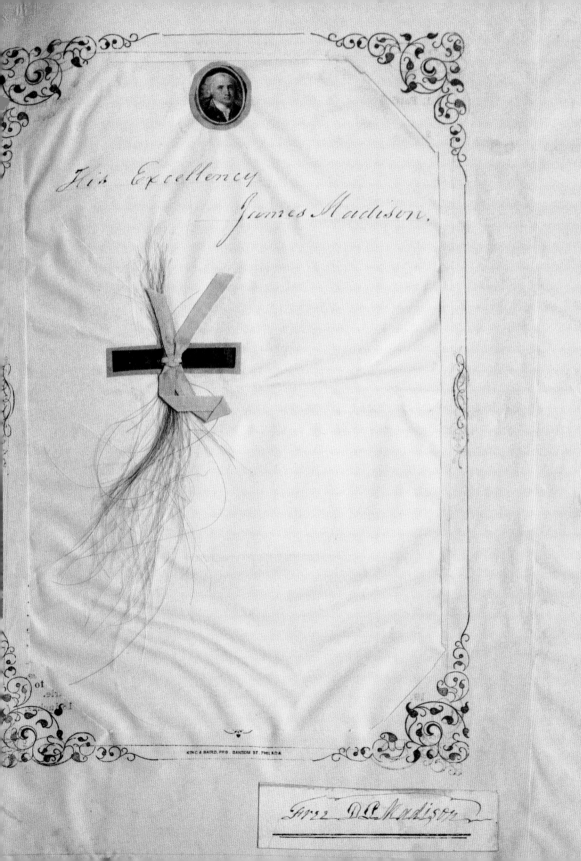

His Excellency

James Madison.

Pres. D.P. Madison

KING & BAIRD, PRS. SANSOM ST. PHILADA.

His Exc

His Ex.y Ja.s Monroe.

ncy.

James Monroe.

-15 p

ma

s a

Man

pos

M.

nac

ar, a

1.

to

na

ny

His Excellency.

John D. Adams.

A. BROWNE'S COLLECTION OF PILE.

His Excellency
Gen Andrew Jackson

His Ex.y Martin Van Buren.

P. A. BROWNE'S COLLECTION OF PILE.

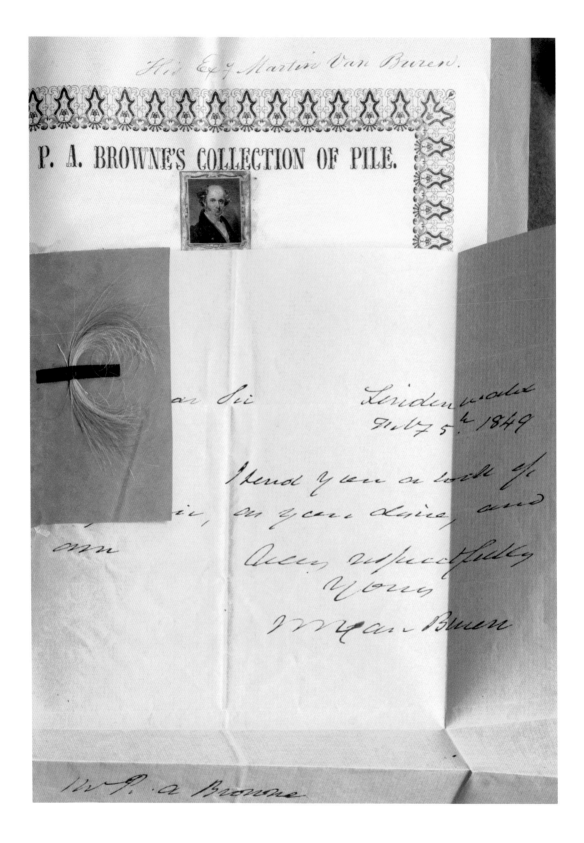

Dear Sir   Lindenwald
                           July 5.th 1849

            I send you a lock of
   hair, as you desire, and
am
            Very respectfully
                    Yours
            M Van Buren

To P. A. Browne

His Excellency
Gen'l W'm Henry
Harrison

Wm H Harrison
Presented by J. Madison Cutts
June 16 th 1853

DUCIT AMOR PATRIÆ.

P. A. BROWNE'S COLLECTION OF PILE.

His Excellency
John Tyler.

A Browne

My dear Sir

I have obtained the loc
red — If you will call on me to morrow
you
yours truly
Thomas Bradford
Feb 7. 1849

Thomas Bradford Esq

DUCIT AMOR PATRIÆ.

James K. Polk

P. A. BROWNE'S COLLECTION OF PILE.

His Excellency Jas. K. Polk.

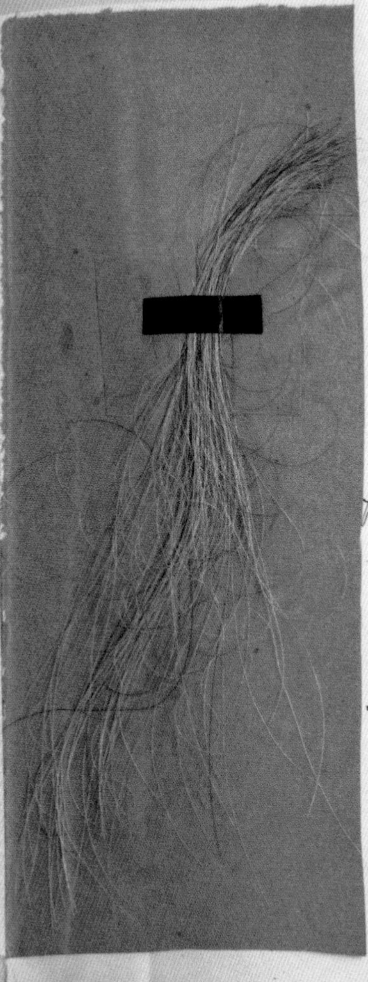

y Dear Sir,

I repeated my search in the very same box
succeeded in finding the enclosed lock of Col. Polk's hair
which conveyed it to me. Take a small portion of the ha
you think it useful as authentication, a copy of the letter
return the rest at your convenience.

Truly & resp. yrs.

G. M. Dakat.

4. Oct. '49

Peter A. Browne Esq.

(Copy.)

Nashville, Tenn June 16 – 1849

D Sir Though personally a stranger to you I h
the liberty of enclosing to you a lock of the deceased e
President Polk's hair, which I took from his head to
for this purpose while assisting in removing locks for his
family. I trust I am not in error in s

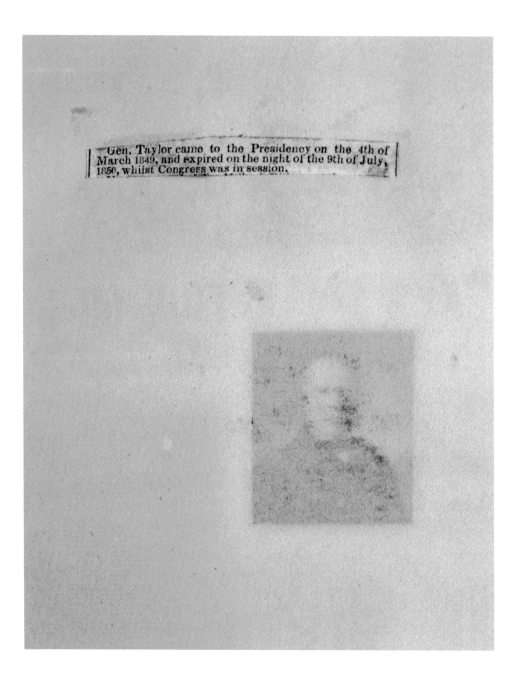

Gen. Taylor came to the Presidency on the 4th of
March 1849, and expired on the night of the 9th of July,
1850, whilst Congress was in session.

P. A. BROWNE'S COLLECTION OF PILE.

His Excellency, Gen
Zachary Taylor.

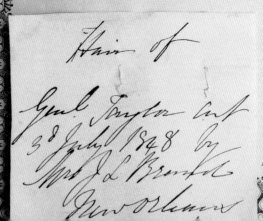

Hair of
Genl. Taylor cut
3d July 1848 by
Mrs J L Brent
New Orleans

AMOR PATRIÆ.

P. A. BROWNE'S COLLECTION OF PILE.

His Ex'y Franklin Pierce

Eng'd by W.B. Hall

Franklin Pierce

PRESIDENT OF THE UNITED STATES.

DUCIT AMOR PATRIÆ.

Y'r Franklin Pierce

Described by his biographer as "the last man who knew everything," Joseph Leidy (1823–1891) was the country's first professional paleontologist, the foremost microscopist in America, and from 1853 until his death a professor of anatomy in the University of Pennsylvania. His 1861 anatomy textbook became the standard anatomical text for medical students for decades.

Leidy wrote extensively on fossils and assembled a nearly complete dinosaur skeleton from bones found in New Jersey. He is also recognized as the father of American parasitology and a pioneer in the application of forensic analysis in America's criminal justice system. He served as a curator and president of the Wagner Free Institute of Science (1885–1891) and the Academy of Natural Sciences of Philadelphia (1881–1891).

P. A. BROWNE'S COLLECTION OF PILE.

Prof. Joseph Leidy.

Artist, naturalist, and museum impresario, Charles Willson Peale (1741–1827) is best known for his portraits of George and Martha Washington, Thomas Jefferson, Benjamin Franklin, and many of the other leaders of the American Revolution, whose hair was later collected by Peter Browne. In 1786 Peale opened Peale's Museum, an institution founded for the public display of a wide range of natural history specimens and other objects. The museum housed Peale's paintings, the first complete skeleton of an American mastodon, taxidermied animals, shells, insects, and minerals. The museum was sold (to P. T. Barnum) in 1849. Sadly, most of its scientific collections were destroyed by fires in 1851 and 1865.

Charles Wilson Peale Esq
the founder of the Philad.
Museum.

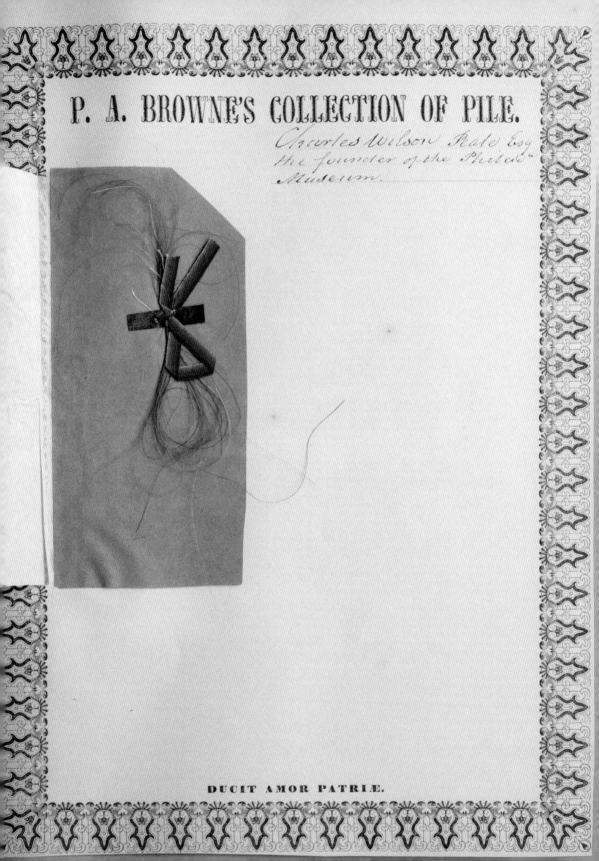

In 1856 Thomas Dent Mütter (1811–1859) wrote to the College of Physicians of Philadelphia that ill health was forcing him to resign his post as professor of surgery at Jefferson Medical College. He also offered the college guardianship of the unique anatomic and pathological materials he had collected for his personal "museum."

Mütter had been appointed to the chair of surgery at Jefferson in 1841, just ten years after receiving his MD degree from the University of Pennsylvania. Following his graduation he spent a year in Paris, the medical Mecca of the period. Mütter returned to the United States with an understanding of the latest French techniques in orthopedic and plastic surgery and a firm belief in a system of teaching medicine based on close observation of actual cases. He amassed a large assortment of specimens for use in his classes. The Mütter Museum in Philadelphia is his legacy to the profession.

P. A. BROWNE'S COLLECTION OF PILE.

Prof. I. D. Müller
Philad.

DUCIT AMOR PATRIÆ.

Dr. James Mease MD of Philadelphia
Born 11th Aug. 1771.

James Mease (1771–1846), scientific thinker and author, was one of Philadelphia's most prominent citizens. Mease served as a hospital surgeon during the War of 1812. He was heavily involved in Philadelphia's intellectual community and published on a wide range of topics, including agriculture, geology, medicine, and prisons. He corresponded sporadically with Thomas Jefferson for many years on agricultural, historical, and scientific topics. Mease was a member and sometime secretary of the Philadelphia Society for Promoting Agriculture and a founder of both the Athenaeum of Philadelphia and the Pennsylvania Horticultural Society. In his *Domestic Encyclopedia* (1804), Mease wrote that "Love Apples," as he called the tomato, made "a fine catsup," and in 1812 he published the first known tomato ketchup recipe.

P. A. BROWNE'S COLLECTION OF PILE.

James Mease M. D.

Dr Mease's

hair

With the respects of Dr Elwyn

DUCIT AMOR PATRIÆ.

Josiah Clark Nott (1804–1873) was an American physician and surgeon who made his medical reputation by determining that yellow fever was a disease spread by mosquitoes and not something emerging from the air. He had a special interest in the subject, as four of his children died from the disease in one week in the disastrous epidemic of 1853.

A slave owner in Mobile, Alabama, Nott was an outspoken proponent of polygenism, the belief that each race had a separate origin. In 1850 he published a book with George R. Gliddon titled *Types of Mankind*, in which he aimed to give scientific justification for his racial bias, citing Peter Browne's hair studies as proof of different origins of race. African Americans, he argued, were destined to permanent inferiority, and some races, such as the American Indians, were doomed to extinction. Although Nott's writings on race were often irrational in content, they were generally accepted by the leading racial theorists of the day in the United States and Europe. When Darwin eventually disproved the theory of polygenism in *The Descent of Man* (1871), Nott gracefully conceded defeat, saying that had he had access to the same information Darwin had, he would not have published his book.

P. A. BROWNE'S COLLECTION OF PILE.

J. C. Nott M.D. of Mobile
Ala 3.

J. C. Nott. Mobile
aged – 44 –

DUCIT AMOR PATRIÆ.

One of America's most influential scientists, Joseph Henry (1797–1878) served from 1846 to 1878 as the first secretary of the Smithsonian Institution, where he developed a program for research and international exchanges, in keeping with James Smithson's bequest for the foundation of an institution "for the increase and diffusion of knowledge."

As a teenager Henry was keen on a career as an actor, but when by chance he read a book of lectures on scientific topics, his interest in science was piqued. Independent of Michael Faraday in England, Henry discovered mutual electromagnetic inductance, and Henry was the first to notice the phenomenon of electromagnetic self-inductance.

His many achievements include building an electromagnet for Yale College that could support 2,063 pounds, setting a world record at the time. He built and operated a telegraph of his own design that worked between his Princeton University (then the College of New Jersey) laboratory and home on the campus (1.5 miles) and he developed the electromagnet into a precursor to the electric doorbell in 1830. He also found that currents could be induced at a distance and in one experiment magnetized a needle by using a lightning flash eight miles away, apparently the first use of radio waves across a distance.

Prof. Joseph Henry.

Smithsonian Institution
Feby 7th 1849

Enclosed I send you
[of] my head which you
[may give] the honor of [wo]
[rthy] a place in your
[collection of] the hair of distinguished
[individua]ls. I should perhaps
[say that] the lock was cut
[re]cently which may make
[a difference] in the moral de
[ductions] which are to be drawn
[from a comparison of] the specimens

[You may] put down my name
[subscriber] for two more copies
[of the book] also place two copies
[in the] name of Dr Buck
[who has] not authorized by [him]
[self] to subscribe in the
[name] of our funds for

James Fenimore Cooper (1789–1851) was one of the most popular nineteenth-century American authors, and his work was admired around the world. Joining the crew of a merchant ship as a common sailor at age seventeen, Cooper saw his first glimpses of England when Britain was in the midst of war with Napoleon's France. In 1808 Cooper's commission as midshipman in the United States Navy was signed by President Jefferson.

Cooper inherited a fortune from his father in 1809 and married two years later. On a bet from his wife, Susan, that he could write a book better than one she was reading, Cooper turned to writing historical romances and other novels. In 1823 he published *The Pioneers*, the first of the *Leatherstocking* series of five novels featuring Natty Bumppo, a resourceful Anglo-American woodsman raised in part by Native Americans. Bumppo was also the main character of Cooper's most famous book, *The Last of the Mohicans* (1826), one of the most widely read American novels of the nineteenth century.

Mr S. Fenimore Cooper.

DEATH OF JAMES FENNIMORE COOPER, THE NO-
VELIST.—James Fennimore Cooper, Esq., died at
Cooperstown, Otsego county, N. Y., on Sunday
last. The event was not unexpected, but will not
be the less regretted. Mr. Cooper has contributed
largely to the amusement of readers wherever the
English language is spoken, and no American has
done more to advance the literary reputation of his
country. Mr. Cooper was born in Burlington
county, N. J., on the 15th September, 1789. He
was 62 years old, lacking a day, at the period of
his death. The foundation of his fame as a novelist
was laid by the production of his Spy, which was
followed up speedily by the Pioneer, and the other
"Leather Stocking" tales and his sea novels. He
produced thirty-four novels, besides a Naval History, Travels &c. A writer in the International
Magazine, in reviewing Mr. Cooper's works, says:
"There was not a language in Europe in which
all his novels, after the publication of the 'Red
Rover,' did not appear almost as soon as they were
printed in London. He has been the chosen com-
panion of the prince and the peasant, on the borders
of the Volga, the Danube, and Guadalquiver; by
the Indus and the Ganges, the Paraguay and the
Amazon, where the same even of Washington was
never spoken, and our country is known only as the
home of Cooper. The world has living no other
writer whose fame is so universal. We may add
that among the early admirers of Cooper as a novelist, was the late Colonel Trumbull, the historical
painter, whom we have heard express his preference for Cooper's novels, even over those of Sir
Walter Scott."

Death of James F. Cooper.   IT AMOR PATRIÆ.
NEW YORK, September 15.—We lea
Cooperstown that James Fennimore Coop
distinguished novelist, died at his residenc
place yesterday, at one o'clock, in the 62
his age.

Thomas Sully (1783–1872) was lauded as the finest portrait painter in Philadelphia and one of the best in the country; his oeuvre comprises well over two thousand portraits. Nearly single-handedly he created the vogue for full-length portraiture in Philadelphia, and his flourishing success had him painting celebrated public figures and fashionable private citizens. He was especially well known for his idealized portraits of women.

Although historical subjects were rare in his work, in 1816 Sully won (over Rembrandt Peale) a commission to paint two full-length portraits of George Washington. In place of the second portrait, Sully suggested, "I think a very excellent historical Portrait might be painted from some well known incident in the Revolutionary War—for instance the passage of the Delaware, preparatory for the Battle of Princeton." The resulting work, completed in 1819, is his best-known painting, *The Passage of the Delaware*. Originally intended for the Senate Hall in Raleigh, North Carolina, it is now owned by the Museum of Fine Arts in Boston.

P. A. BROWNE'S COLLECTION OF PILE.

Thomas Sully Esq.

DUCIT AMOR PATRIÆ.

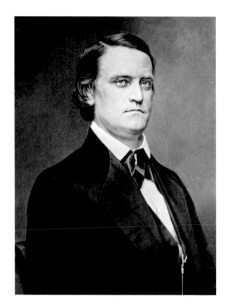

After an errant youth, Robert Jefferson Breckinridge (1800–1871), son
of a Kentucky senator, became a politician and a Presbyterian minister. He supported interdependence between the states over states'
rights, and as conflict leading to the Civil War escalated, he supported
the Union and called for an end to slavery even though he was himself a slave owner. As superintendent of public education, he achieved
impressive reform to the Kentucky educational system: in 1840 only one
of every ten school-age children in Kentucky ever attended school; by
1850 only one out of every ten school-age children did not attend school.

J. Breckenridge

From, Robert J. Breckinridge, of Ky,
Minister of the Gospel.

Ætatis, 55 years, and 7 months: very full
suit, and no tendency to baldness.
Breadalbane, near Lexington,
October 13th 1855.
☞ see inclosure

Elias Hicks (1748–1830) was a powerful and popular traveling Quaker minister from Long Island, New York, whose doctrine of obedience to the Inner Light impressed Walt Whitman when he heard him preach in Brooklyn. Hicks was an early, thoroughly uncompromising abolitionist and the author of *Observations on the Slavery of Africans and Their Descendants* (1811). He identified financial profit as the principal reason for the perpetuation of slavery and advocated a consumer boycott of slave-produced goods. The abolitionist and women's rights activist Lydia Maria Child (1802–1880) reported that Hicks's dying concern was that no cotton blanket, a product of slavery, should cover him on his deathbed.

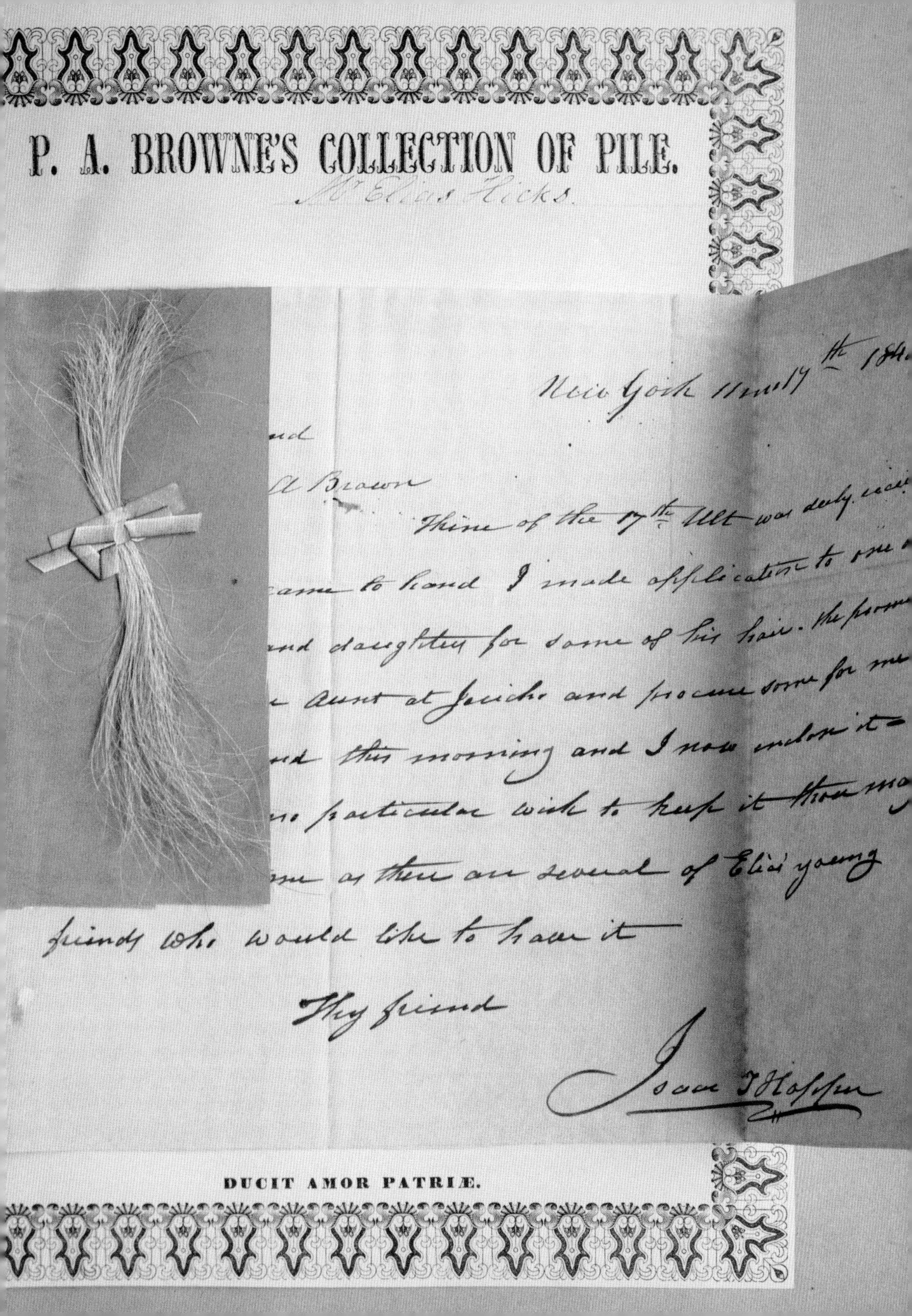

P. A. BROWNE'S COLLECTION OF PILE.
Mr Elias Hicks
New York 11mo 17th 184
nd
A Brown
Thine of the 17th Ult was duly rec
came to hand I made application to one
and daughter for some of his hair. the former
e aunt at Jericho and procure some for me
nd this morning and I now enclose it
no particular wish to keep it thou ma
me as there are several of Elias young
friends who would like to have it
Thy friend
Isaac T Hopper
DUCIT AMOR PATRIÆ.

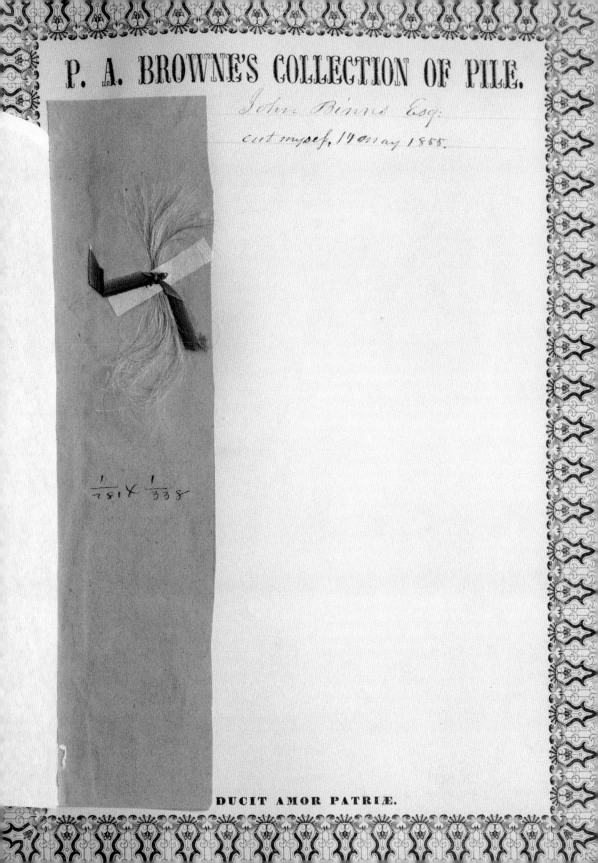

John Binns Esq.

cut myself, 14 May 1855.

$$\frac{1}{781} \times \frac{1}{338}$$

Philada. May 11- 1855.

My dear old & faithful friend,
tried in the fiery furnace of party politics
yet never found wanting. Your visit
yesterday was, after a long absence heart-cheering.
Time has been doing his work upon both of us.
I regretted to see you, the younger of the two by
thirty years the most downhearted in Spirit and
not the most vigorous in health. Look back my
friend upon the actions of a very useful and active
life devoted for the most part to objects to promote
the public welfare, when our remains shall be
mouldering in their silent graves your useful
labors will be felt and understood. Cheer up then and
be as you say I am not only content but cheerful
    With the very best wishes for you and
Yours Boeman your Friend
            John Binns.

Peter A. Browne Esq

John Binns (1772–1860) was one of a number of expatriate Irishmen
key to the development of a militant radicalism in 1790s England, influ-
enced by the French Revolution and the insurrectionary politics of
Tom Paine. Binns was tried for treason in 1798, and although he was
not convicted, he was later imprisoned without charge for almost two
years in Gloucester jail, after which he immigrated to the United States
in 1801. He settled in Philadelphia, where he established a popular
newspaper, the *Democratic Press*, and served as an alderman from
1822 to 1844.

Winfield Scott (1786–1866), known as "Old Fuss and Feathers" for his insistence on military discipline and appearance, was the foremost American military figure between the Revolution and the Civil War. He first distinguished himself in combat in the War of 1812 and by age twenty-seven was promoted to brigadier general. In the 1830s, he was in command during the Indian Wars in the West and oversaw the infamous Cherokee removal, the Trail of Tears, in 1838. Promoted to major general in 1841, he led American forces in Mexico in 1846 during the Mexican-American War, earning him such recognition that in 1852, the Whig Party passed over its own incumbent president, Millard Fillmore to nominate Scott as the party's candidate in that year's presidential election. At the start of the American Civil War, he conceived a strategy for the Union to crush the Confederacy slowly. Though derided as the Anaconda Plan, the actual Union victory followed its broad outlines. When Scott retired in 1861, his military career had spanned fifty-three years, forty-seven of which were as a general, and three major wars.

P. A. BROWNE'S COLLECTION OF PILE.

Maj. Gen. Winfield Scott.

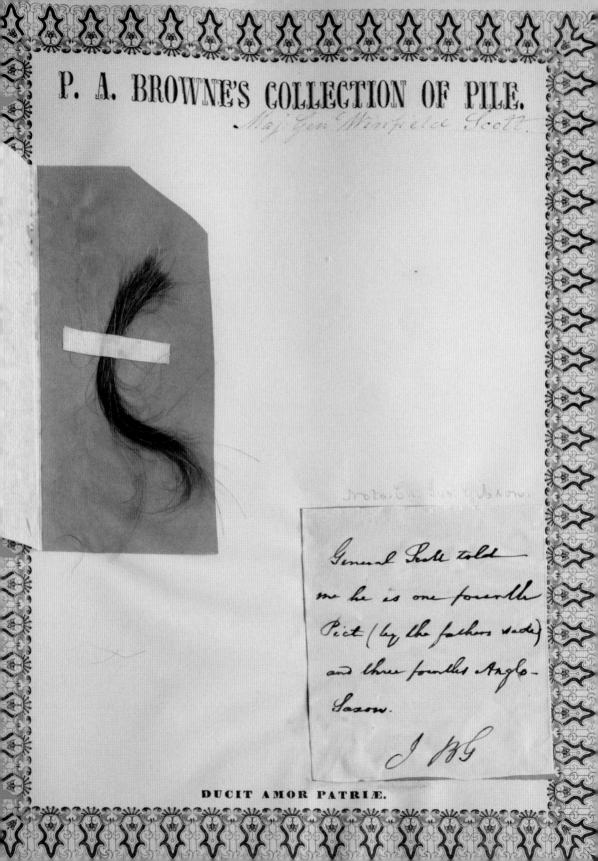

General Scott told
me he is one fourth
Pict (by the fathers side)
and three fourths Anglo-
Saxon.

J H G

DUCIT AMOR PATRIÆ.

Major Wm Jackson Aid
to Genl Washington.

Colonel James Page (1795–1875) was a veteran of the War of 1812 and an illustrious figure in Philadelphia. Having received only a rudimentary log cabin education, in Bucks County, Pennsylvania, he became an office boy with Peter A. Browne and, by advice of his employer, became a law student. He was admitted to practice at age twenty-one. A member of the Philadelphia Bar, Page held many public positions throughout his life, including president of the Hibernia Fire Company, the postmaster of Philadelphia, president of the Democratic State Association, commissioner for the erection of new public buildings, collector of the port of Philadelphia, and commissioner of bankruptcy. He was also a prominent member of the Philadelphia Skating Club and for a long time known as the "Prince of Skaters." In Philadelphia and Atlantic City, Page was prominently identified with art matters and social entertainments.

P. A. BROWNE'S COLLECTION OF PILE.

A. James Page

Sep: 1855.

Ethnology

Ethnology is a branch of anthropology that examines the origin, distribution, and distinguishing characteristics of human societies. Originating in Europe at the end of the eighteenth century, it took on a life of its own in the United States in the early nineteenth century.

Peter Browne's focus on human hair as a means of understanding ethnographic diversity may seem controversial by twenty-first century standards. It is, however, less troubling than the efforts of the comparative anatomist Samuel Morton and his fellow physical anthropologists during the same period who assembled worldwide collections of human skulls to compare their cranial capacity and other physical attributes.

Browne acknowledged that his ideas about ethnic diversity might contain flaws, and he invited dialogue and corrections from anyone with differing views or understanding. A man of his time, he drew conclusions about other cultures that we would not today, but he built an irreplaceable mass of material in his relentless pursuit of knowledge. The hair samples he gathered form a unique historical collection as fascinating as it is disquieting, with important ramifications for generations to come.

National.

INDIAN

HAIR.

P. A. BROWNE'S COLLECTION OF PILE.

*Pure Arrawaack
Indian Female.
presented by Heren
tes of Surinam or Dutch
Guiana, So. Am.*

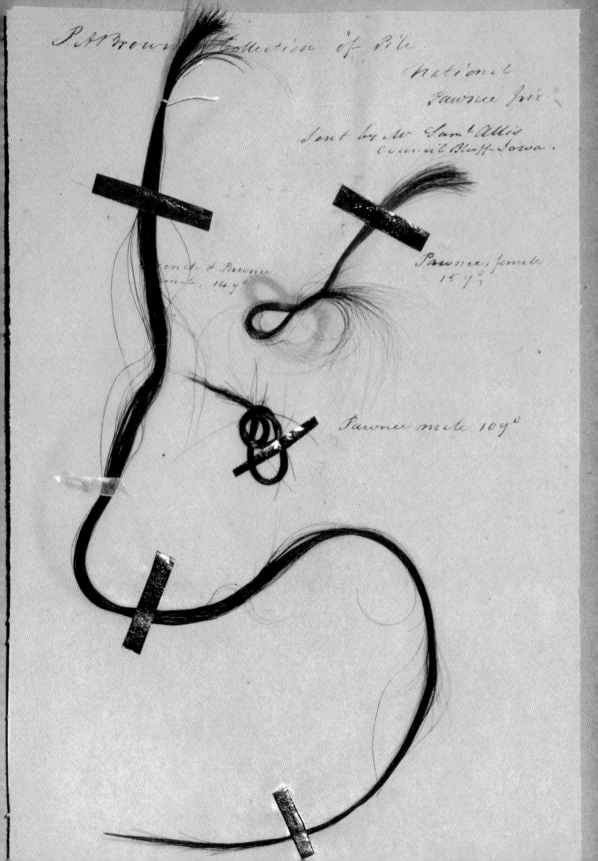

P.H. Brown Collection of Pile.

National
Pawnee Ind.

Sent by Mr Sam'l Allis
Council Bluff, Iowa.

French & Pawnee
male, 14 y[?]

Pawnee, female
15 y[?]

Pawnee male 10 y[?]

B. Browne's Collection of Pile.

Winnebago Indian
said to be *illegible*

Mee un Kaw
Winnebago female
no complexion dark
black eyes

a Slave of Mr Jno H. Hundley had three
ren at a birth, — 2 black & one white.

P. A. BROWNE'S COLLECTION OF PILE.

Father & Mother
pure negroes

Black Child.
pure negro

White Child.
Black Albinos.

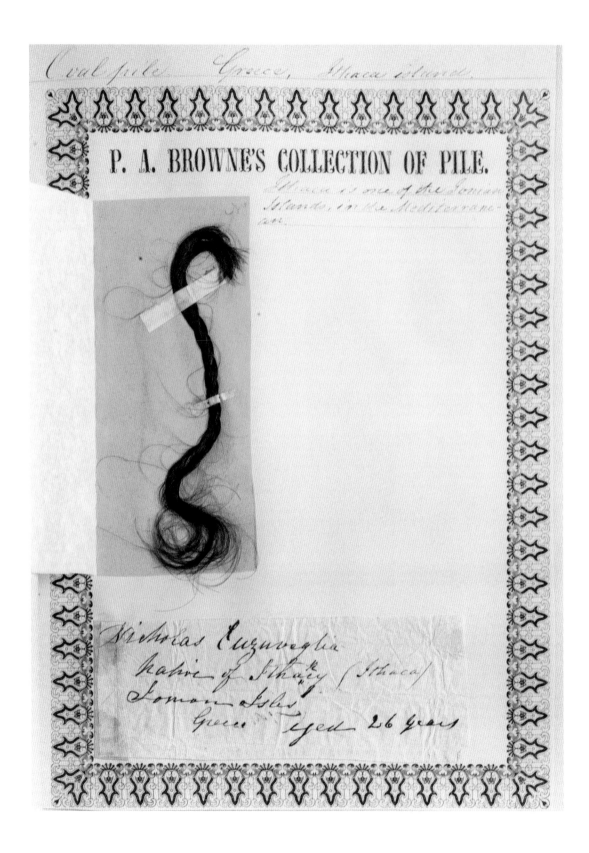

Oval pile. Greece, Ithaca island.

P. A. BROWNE'S COLLECTION OF PILE.

Ithaca is one of the Ionian
Islands, in the Mediterran-
ean.

Nicholas Euzuveglia
Native of Ithaky (Ithaca)
Ionian Isles
Greece Aged 26 years

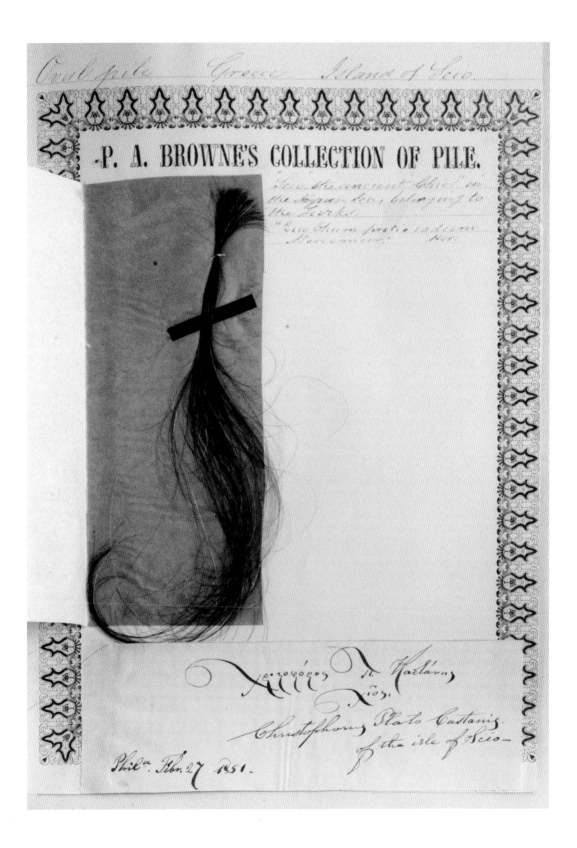

Oval pile   Greece   Island of Scio.

P. A. BROWNE'S COLLECTION OF PILE.

Scio, the ancient Chios in
the Ægean Sea, belonging to
the Turks.

"Quo suum pretio caderem
Mercenarii."   Hor.

Θεοδόρος Π. Καστάνης,
Χίος.

Christopheros Plato Castanis
of the isle of Scio—

Phila. Febr. 27 1851.

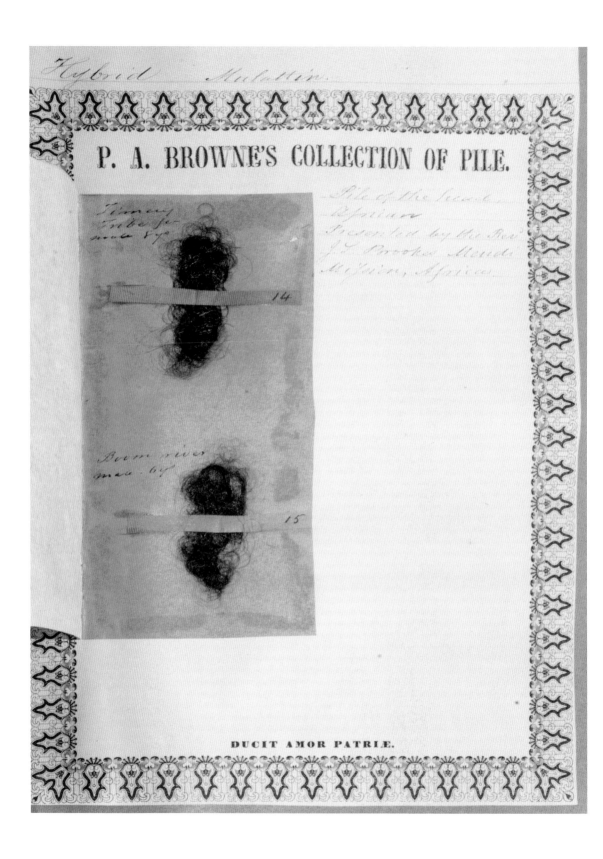

P. A. BROWNE'S COLLECTION OF PILE.

Pile of the head
African
Presented by the Rev.
J. S. Brooke Mende
Africa, Africa

Timney
Tribe fe-
male 87°

14

Boom river
male 64

15

DUCIT AMOR PATRIÆ.

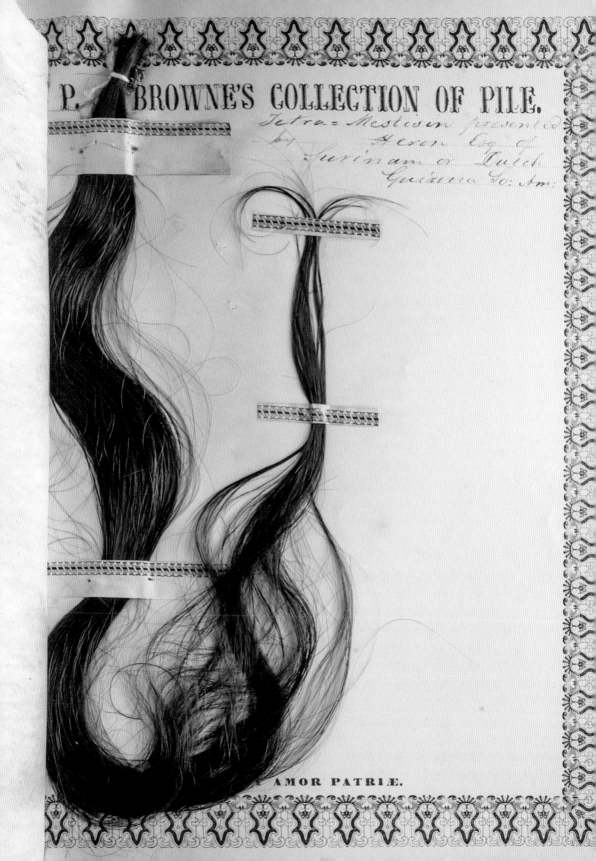

P. BROWNE'S COLLECTION OF PILE.

Tetra = Mestiesin presented by ____ Heern Esq of Surinam or Dutch Guiana So: Am:

AMOR PATRIÆ.

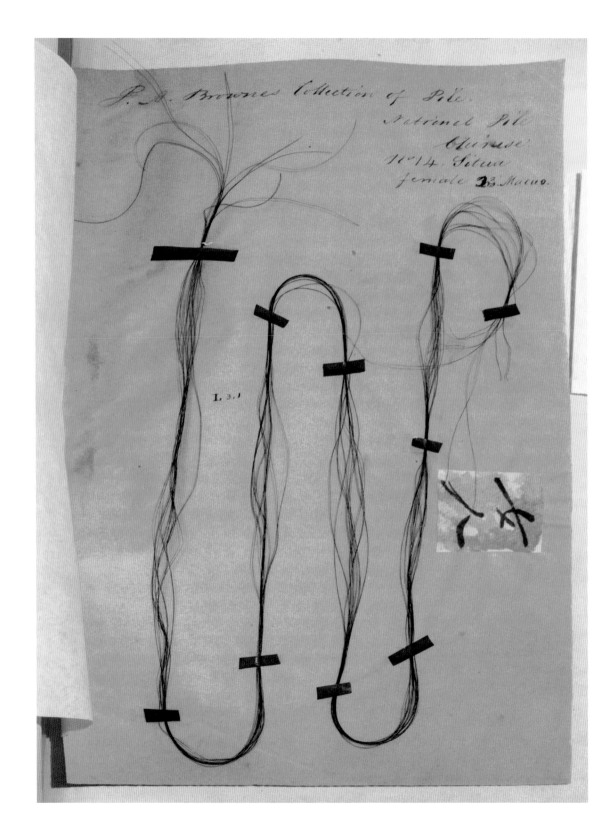

P. A. Browne's Collection of Pile.

Natural Pile
Chinese:
N°14. Situa
female 23. Macuo.

I, 3, 1

Chinese
presented by Lieut. Jr.
Jones.

Asia
Chinese Steward
on the U. S. Rev. Schooner
Hamilton
Hair with
his card

P. A. BROWNE'S COLLECTION OF PILE.

Neck ornaments of human hair from Penrhyns Islands

U.S. Ex. Exp. Glt Wilkes U.S.N. Com

DUCIT AMOR PATRIÆ.

P. A. BROWNE'S COLLECTION OF PILE.

New Zealand Chief
D.r Pickering
Pekea of Taranaka
Nohhoohee Tribe
            see Wilkes Nar?"

U.S. Ex. Exp.n Charles
Wilkes U.S.N Com.d,

DUCIT AMOR PATRIÆ.

P. A. BROWNE'S COLLECTION OF PILE.

Pile of the Zulus or Amazulus, a branch of the Kaffers of South Africa. Collected for P. A. Browne by the Rev. Lewis Grout, Missionary to the Zulu Tribes near Port Natal on the Eastern Coast of Africa, at the instance of Prof. Chauncey A. Goodrich of New Haven, Connecticut. 1855 — (see letter)

Latham, (in his work on the varieties of Man,) thus describes the Southern Kaffres.

Cranium more vaulted & less prognathic than the Negro; hair tufted, & as such approaching that of the Hottentot; if geometric development, outward, rather than downward, so that the cheek bones become projecting & the forehead & chin tapering; lips generally thick, & nasal profile less generally depressed than with the negro; color black, dark brown, & clear brown; stature tall.

DUCIT AMOR PATRIÆ.

P. A. BROWNE'S COLLECTION OF PILE.

back — Umxahon aged 50. of
the Amanyeeswa Tribe.
Note. He had none on his
head.

Chest

Beard

Cheek

Hair &c of Umxahon
of the amanyeeswa
tribe — aged about
50 — (no hair for the head)
— only for the back, chest
& cheek &c
L. Grout.

P. A. BROWNE'S COLLECTION OF PILE.

Israelitish hair.

Jacob Greenbaum aged 53.
born at Bavaria.

2 Michael Cracker
aged 7. from Poland
near the Russian
boundary.

3 Ethesa Colesbury
aged 18.
from Mainesbury
Germany.

DUCIT AMOR PATRIÆ.

P. A. BROWNE'S COLLECTION OF PILE.

Israelitish hair

11 Aadolph Benbaum aged 32
born at Furtt.

12 Heiman Heiman aged
20 born at Tiefenbach.

9 Carl Weiler
aged 72 born
in Steinberg.

13 Abm Buchheifer aged 28
born in Bavaria.

DUCIT AMOR PATRIÆ.

P. A. BROWNE'S COLLECTION OF PILE.

Peter A. Browne
L L D. of Philad⁰.
aged 73.

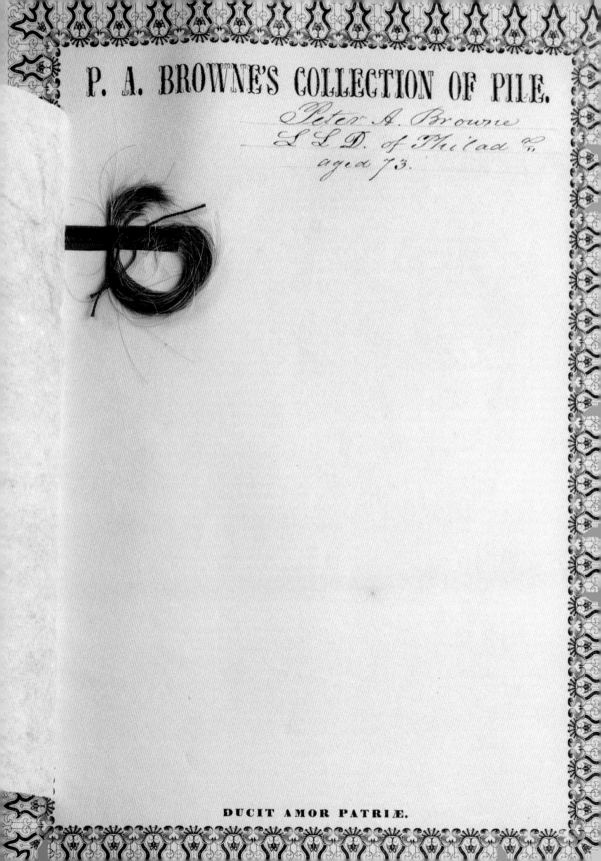

DUCIT AMOR PATRIÆ.

NOTES

1. "Pile" is derived from the Latin word for hair, *pilus*. Browne refers to his "national collection" in various letters requesting specimens. See correspondence file, Browne Pile Collections, Academy of Natural Sciences of Philadelphia (ANSP), Drexel University, coll. 756.

2. Browne's first published discussion of these differences appeared in a journal called *The Plough, the Loom and the Anvil* in 1850. Cited in Browne's *Trichologia Mammalium, or A Treatise on the Organization, Properties and Uses of Hair and Wool, Together with an Essay Upon the Raising and Breeding of Sheep* (Philadelphia: J. H. Jones, 1853), p. 155.

3. Browne, *Trichologia Mammalium*, p. 158.

4. In *Trichologia Mammalium*, Browne said the word was derived from "trix," or hair. See ibid., preface and p. 57.

5. For a description of Browne's "trichometer" illustrated here, see ibid., p. 57.

6. Philadelphia Society for Promoting Agriculture files, MS 92, box 1, folder 24, Van Pelt Library, University of Pennsylvania.

7. "Scientific Examinations," *Philadelphia Ledger and Transcript*, March 7, 1849, in Browne correspondence file, ANSP coll. 756.

8. Eric Stoykovich, "The Culture of Improvement in the Early Republic: Domestic Livestock, Animal Breeding, and Philadelphia's Urban Gentlemen, 1820–1860," *Pennsylvania Magazine of History and Biography*, vol. CXXXIV, no. 1 (January 2010): 51–52.

9. Browne's wool display won an Honorable Mention at the exhibition. *Great Exhibition of the Works of Industry of All Nations, 1851, Reports by the Juries on the Subjects on the Thirty Classes into which the Exhibition was Divided* (London: Spicer Bros., 1852), pp. 157–59. *Great Exhibition of the Works of Industry of All Nations, Official Descriptive and Illustrated Catalogue in Three Volumes; vol. III: Foreign States* (London: Spicer Bros., 1851), pp. 1431–35.

10. "Exhibition of American Wool at the World's Exhibition," *Plough, the Loom and the Anvil* 6 (1854): 582; "American Wool in England," *New England Farmer* 7 (1855): 452; "American Wool in England," *Southern Planter* 15 (1855): 383.

11. *Minutes of the Farmers Club of Pennsylvania, A Record of Seventy Years, 1849–1919* (Philadelphia: privately printed by J. B. Lippincott Co., 1920), entry for meeting on January 21, 1852, pp. 31–32.

12. A major American sheep breeder named Mark Cockrill (1788–1872), who had contributed wool samples to Browne's collection from his plantations in Tennessee and Mississippi, won a "Prize Medal" for his wool at the Crystal Palace exhibition. Cockrill also had a collection of wool samples, but these were limited to his own sheep, while Browne's collection was worldwide in scope. Except for the ones in Browne's collection, Cockrill's wool samples are no longer known to exist. I am grateful to Eric C. Stoykovich, who researched Cockrill's sheep breeding activities for his PhD dissertation at the University of Virginia (2009), for generously sharing this information.

13. P. A. Browne and M. W. Dickeson, *Trichographia Mammalium, or Descriptions and Drawings of the Hairs of the Mammalia, Made with the Aid of the Microscope* (Philadelphia: J. H. Jones, 1848).

14. Ibid.

15. Browne, *Trichologia Mammalium*, p. 56.

16. Ibid., p. 138.

17. Ibid.

18. Browne appears to have been successful in publishing only his findings on the opossum. See Browne and Dickeson, *Trichographia Mammalium*.

19. P. A. Browne, solicitation form letter printed ca. 1850.

20. Assisting Wilkes in this effort was Dr. Charles Pickering (1805–1878), a member of the U.S. Exploring Expedition and the author of the fifteenth volume of its report, *Races of Man and Their*

Geographical Distribution (1851). For Pickering's diary of the expedition, see ANSP collection 308. For an overview of the expedition and its purpose, see Nathaniel Philbrick, *Sea of Glory: America's Voyage of Discovery, the U.S. Exploring Expedition 1838–1842* (New York: Viking, 2003).

21. Browne and Dickeson, *Trichographia Mammalium.*

22. In an "advertisement" in *Trichographia Mammalium* (1848) in which he requested samples of human hair, Browne wrote, "Wherever practical, the follicle or root should be obtained." In his solicitation form letter, Browne said, "When the specimen [of human hair] is *cut* from the head, it ought to be accompanied by a few hairs *drawn out,* (not cut,) to enable me to examine the *button,* which is generally extracted with the shaft." For the purposes of DNA analysis, the additional information he requested is extremely helpful.

23. Browne and Dickeson, *Trichographia Mammalium.*

24. Browne, solicitation form letter.

25. See letter from P. A. Browne to J. F. Cooper, April 25, 1849, Cooper collection, Beinecke Rare Book and Manuscript Library, Yale University. The correspondence with the others mentioned or their families is associated with Browne's albums, ANSP coll. 756. Although Browne prepared a page for Jefferson Davis, then secretary of war, complete with a portrait, he was never successful in obtaining a sample of his hair.

26. Browne, solicitation form letter.

27. The hair Browne collected was mounted, sometimes with portraits of the donors, in albums whose pages were embellished with a classical border and identified as "P. A. Browne's Collection of Pile." To reinforce their importance, some of the sheets also bore the patriotic slogan DUCIT AMOR PATRIAE ("Led by love of country").

28. Letters from James Buchanan to Peter Browne, October 6, 1849, and February 25, 1850, Browne correspondence file, ANSP coll. 756.

29. Browne correspondence file, ANSP coll. 756.

30. The Arctic explorer Elisha Kent Kane sent Browne hair samples from the Inuit he encountered. The missionaries with whom he communicated were also extremely helpful. See William Stanton, *The Leopard's Spots: Scientific Attitudes Toward Race in America, 1815–1859* (Chicago: University of Chicago Press, 1960), p. 153.

31. Joseph Henry to Peter A. Browne, December 14, 1855, Browne correspondence file, ANSP coll. 756.

32. Ibid.

33. Stanton, *The Leopard's Spots*, p. 153.

34. The donor of Napoleon's hair was identified by Browne as Prof. John K. Mitchell of Philadelphia in *Classification of Mankind by the Hair and Wool of Their Heads* (Philadelphia: J. H. Jones, 1852), p. 5. According to Browne's notes in album 3 of his collection (ANSP coll. 756), Mitchell had obtained the specimen from Napoleon's "English surgeon at St. Helena." This could have been one of three people: Barry O'Meara (1786–1836), who served as Napoleon's physician from 1815 to 1818; John Stokoe (1775–1852), a military doctor who served as his physician in 1818; or, most likely, Archibald Arnott (1772–1855), a military doctor who attended Napoleon during the final weeks of his life in 1821. For more on Napoleon's doctors, see Ben Weider and David Hapgood, *The Murder of Napoleon* (New York: Congdon & Lattes, 1982).

35. Peter Brown, *The Cult of the Saints: Its Rise and Function in Latin Christianity* (Chicago: University of Chicago Press, 1981).

36. Cynthia Hahn, *Strange Beauty—Issues in the Making and Meaning of Reliquaries 400–circa 1204* (University Park, PA: Pennsylvania State University Press, 2012), p. 136. A novel that revolves around the sometimes real, sometimes fraudulent nature of relic collecting in the Renaissance was published in 2015. See Christopher Buckley, *The Relic Master* (New York: Simon and Schuster, 2015).

37. British Museum, coll. # PE 1902,0625.1.

38. Martina Bagnoli, Holger A. Klein, C. Griffith Mann, and James Robinson, eds., *The Treasures*

of Heaven: Saints, Relics, and Devotion in Medieval Europe (New Haven: Yale University Press, 2010), p. 127.

39. A sample of Beethoven's hair, collected by his fellow composer Ferdinand Hiller on the day of his funeral, is now at the Ira F. Brilliant Center for Beethoven Studies in San Jose, California. A lock of Amelia Earhart's childhood hair is at the Houghton Library, Harvard University; see Cara Giaimo, "Untangling the Secrets of One of Harvard's Historic Hair Collections," *Atlas Obscura*, November 20, 2017. Charlemagne's tomb was opened by Emperor Otto III (r. 996–1002), who found the body completely intact. His hair and fingernails were removed and saved; see Bagnoli et al., *The Treasures of Heaven*, p. 23. John Wilkes Booth's hair is owned by John Reznikoff of Westport, Connecticut; see Jerry Guo, "A Little off the Top for History," *New York Times*, July 13, 2008.

40. For information about and an illustration of the Dürer hair, see Bagnoli et al., *The Treasures of Heaven,* p. 215 and p. 214, fig. 70. The Isabella Stewart Gardner Museum hair specimens are as follows: Liszt: Urn9.ab; Browning: M27e57; Hawthorne: U3n204.a-c.

41. B. Foulon, ed., *Dominique Vivant Denon: L'oeil de Napoleon* (Paris: Musée du Louvre, 2000), p. 480.

42. The coffin-shaped box was made with the oak from Captain Cook's ship HMS *Resolution* by an anonymous member of his crew. See Benjamin Breen, "The Miniature Coffin of Captain Cook," *Atlas Obscura*, October 14, 2013. The envelope containing the Burke hair reads "Burke's Hair Cut off with a Penknife previous to internment—EJW." It was purchased by the State Library in 1941. For more on the Burke hair specimen, see Susan O'Flahertie, ed., *Celebrating 100 Years of the Mitchell Library* (Sydney: Focus Publishing, 2000), p. 155.

43. For a thorough discussion of the popularity of Washington's hair, see Robert McCracken Peck, "George Washington's Brush with Immortality: The Hair Relics of a Sainted Hero," *Antiques* (July–August 2015): 124–31.

44. *Letters and Recollections of George Washington Being Letters of Tobias Lear and Others between 1790 and 1799* (New York: Doubleday, Page, 1906), p. 139.

45. Browne identified the source of his Washington hair sample in his *Classification of Mankind by the Hair and Wool of Their Heads*, p. 5. Note: Pierie's name is sometimes spelled Pierrie, Perrie (as Browne spelled it), and occasionally, based on oral transmission, Perry. For the location of other Washington hair samples collected by Pierie, see Peck, "George Washington's Brush with Immortality."

46. In *Trichologia Mammalium* Browne compared the weight, durability, and elasticity of President Washington's hair with that of presidents Madison and Jackson, but also with the hair of an elephant, a sloth, a grizzly bear, an elk, and a Siberian mammoth (see page 56). The collection of hair samples as memento mori (literally "remember you must die") dates from the sixteenth and seventeenth centuries. See Mary Brett, *Fashionable Mourning Jewelry, Clothing, and Customs* (Atglen, PA: Schiffer, 2006), p. 111. The only other American collector who focused so heavily on U.S. presidents was John Varden, of Washington, D.C., who began collecting presidential hair in 1850. His collection containing hair samples from the first fourteen presidents (George Washington to Franklin Pierce) was framed and displayed at the U.S. Patent Office in 1853. It is now owned by the Smithsonian. Unlike Browne, Varden had no scientific motive for collecting. His was a purely patriotic collection.

47. Stephen Decatur, *Private Affairs of George Washington from the Records and Accounts of Tobias Lear, Esq.* (Boston: Houghton Mifflin, 1933), p. 66.

48. In an order to the English retailer Robert Cary Jr. on August 20, 1770, the Washingtons requested "A Locket with the Inclosed hair in it"

(invoice, August 20, 1770), John Fitzpatrick, ed., *The Writings of George Washington*, 39 volumes (Washington, D.C.: U.S. Government Printing Office, 1931–44), 3:24 and 25.

49. Letter from John James Audubon to Lucy Audubon, December 22, 1826, Field Museum of Natural History, quoted in Alice Ford, ed., *The 1826 Journal of John James Audubon* (New York: Abbeville Press, 1967), p. 413.

50. See Weider and Hapgood, *The Murder of Napoleon*, p. 14.

51. Emily Dickinson letter to Emily Ford, ca. 1845, in *Letters of Emily Dickinson*, Mabel Todd Loomis, ed., vol. 1 (Boston: Roberts Bros., 1894), p. 241, quoted in Helen Sheumaker, *Love Entwined: The Curious History of Hairwork in America* (Philadelphia: University of Pennsylvania Press, 2007), p. 160.

52. Brett, *Fashionable Mourning Jewelry*; and Sheumaker, *Love Entwined*.

53. Mark Campbell, *Self Instructor in the Art of Hair Work* (Berkeley: Lacis, 1989 [1875]), p. 11.

54. Ibid., p. 12.

55. Joseph Henry to P. A. Browne, March 19, 1858. Browne correspondence file, ANSP coll. 756.

56. John Binns to P. A. Browne, May 11, 1855. Browne correspondence file, ANSP coll. 756.

57. Browne, solicitation form letter.

58. Both are in volume 8 of Browne's collection.

59. Julia Pastrana was described in an accompanying broadside as an "Opate Indian" and "Misnomered Bear Woman." "These remarkable beings inhabit the Sierra Madre Mountains in the State of Sinaloa, near California," reports the printed text. "They live in caves, in a naked state, and subsist on grass, roots, insects, barks of trees, &c." The hair, collected on December 5, 1855, is contained in volume 8 of Browne's collection.

60. The Menominee are part of the Algonquian language family of North America, made up of several tribes now located around the Great Lakes and many other tribes based along the Atlantic coast. They are among the historical tribes of present-day upper Michigan and Wisconsin. The hair was sent to Browne by the Rev. B. Phillips of Wisconsin on May 30, 1857, with a letter identifying Black Hawk as "a pure blooded Indian, age about 36 or 40." Browne correspondence file, ANSP coll. 756. The hair sample is in volume 8.

61. The twins' hair was sent to Browne by H. H. Kline on March 30, 1854, along with "a Book containing their history." Browne correspondence file, ANSP coll. 756. The hair sample is in volume 8.

62. These are all in volume 8, ANSP coll. 756. See also Browne's *Trichologia Mammalium*, p. 56.

63. Stanton, *The Leopard's Spots*, pp. 48–49.

64. Luke Burke, introduction to George Gliddon, *Otia Aegyptiaca: Discourses on Egyptian Archaeology and Hieroglyphical Discoveries* (London: James Madden, 1849), pp. 5–6.

65. Stanton, *The Leopard's Spots*, p. 49.

66. Ibid.

67. Ibid., p. 46.

68. Browne had come to know Morton through their shared membership in the Academy of Natural Sciences of Philadelphia. Both George Gliddon and Peter Browne were elected to membership in the Academy in 1841. Morton had a much longer association with the Academy, having been elected a member in 1820. He served as the Academy's recording secretary (1825–1829), curator (1830–31), corresponding secretary (1831–40), vice president (1840–49), and president from 1849 until his death in 1851. For more on Gliddon and Morton, see Robert McCracken Peck and Patricia Tyson Stroud, *A Glorious Enterprise: The Academy of Natural Sciences of Philadelphia and the Making of American Science* (Philadelphia: University of Pennsylvania Press, 2012), pp. 90–106. See also Ann Fabian, *The Skull Collectors: Race, Science, and America's Unburied Dead* (Chicago: University of Chicago Press, 2010).

69. P. A. Browne "communication" in *Proceedings of the Academy of Natural Sciences of Philadelphia*, February 1851, p. 145.

70. Browne, *Trichologia Mammalium*, p. 66. Browne also references the "three distinct species of men" on p. 59.

71. Browne, *The Classification of Mankind by the Hair and Wool of Their Heads, with an answer to Dr. Prichard's Assertion, that 'The Covering of the Head of the Negro Is Hair . . . and not Wool,'* Philadelphia, 1850, p. 8.

72. See Bruce Dain, *A Hideous Monster of the Mind: American Race Theory in the Early Republic* (Cambridge, MA: Harvard University Press, 2003), chaps. 2 and 7; and Thomas Gossett, *Race: The History of an Idea in America* (Dallas, TX: Southern Methodist University Press, 1963). See also Walter Johnson, "The Slave Trader, the White Slave, and the Politics of Racial Determination in the 1850s," *Journal of American History* 87, no. 1 (June 2000). Browne's important role in the split between the monogenists, who believed all humans descended from a single origin, and the polygenists, who believed each racial group had descended separately, is discussed by Sarah Erina Gold McBride in chapter 4 of her 2017 PhD dissertation, "Whiskerology: Hair and the Legible Body in the Nineteenth Century," eSholarship.org, California Digital Library, University of California.

73. For more on this, see Stanton, *The Leopard's Spots*. See also Lester D. Stephens, *Science, Race, and Religion in the American South* (Chapel Hill: University of North Carolina Press, 2000).

74. Browne solicitation form letter.

75. Browne and Dickeson, *Trichographia Mammalium*.

76. Ibid.

77. Because Jefferson had no direct male descendants, researchers have suggested testing his DNA from samples of his hair that survive in the Library of Congress, at Monticello, and from Peter Browne's collection at the Academy of Natural Sciences. See James Breig, "Hair's Breadth: Locks Could be Keys to Jefferson Mystery," *Colonial Williamsburg Journal*, vol. XXXII, no. 3 (Autumn 2010): 60–65. An analysis of samples of Napoleon's hair from museums in Italy and France in 2008 concluded that while the arsenic content was high, it may not have been the cause of his death. See "Scientists Prove Napoleon Not Poisoned," Reuters and MSNBC.com, February 12, 2008. For more on the study of Napoleon's hair as a determinate for his possible arsenic poisoning, see Weider and Hapgood, *The Murder of Napoleon*.

78. Nicholas Wade, "Australian Aborigine Hair Tells a Story of Human Migration," *New York Times*, September 22, 2011.

79. Ibid.

80. Ibid.

81. Ibid.

82. Nicholas Wade, "Lock of Hair Opens Door Onto a Culture's Origins," *New York Times*, May 30, 2008. See also Eske Willerslev et al., *Science* (May 29, 2008), and his 2010 article on Paleo-Eskimo migration in *Nature*, as well as his November 20, 2013, article in *Nature* discussing a 24,000-year-old Siberian boy linking western Europe to Native Americans. See also "A Genomic History of Aboriginal Australia," *Nature* 538 (October 13, 2016): 207–14.

83. Faye Flam, "Hair Creates Picture of an Ancient Man," *Philadelphia Inquirer*, February 15, 2010.

84. http://www.kansascity.com/opinion /opn-columns-blogs/syndicated-columnists /article105647021.html.

CHAPTER IX.

PLATE I.

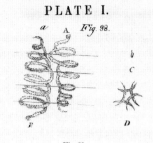

Fig. 99.

THE WOOLLY SHEEP.

Fig. 100.

THE HAIRY SHEEP.

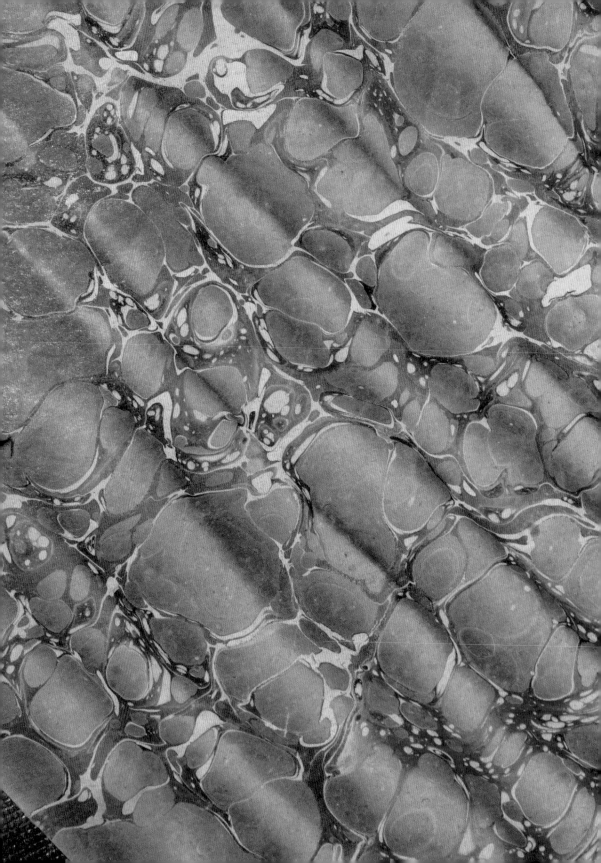